*May Gods
abide in y*

FLASHBACKS

Prisoner of War in the Philippines

J Walter Middleton

T. Walter Middleton
Foreword by Ralph Roberts

Publisher: Ralph Roberts
Vice-President: Pat Roberts

Editor: Pat Roberts

Cover Design: Gayle Graham
Interior Design & Electronic Page Assembly: **WorldComm®**
Photographs as indicated

Copyright©2000, 2001 T. Walter Middleton

Reproduction and translation of any part of this work beyond that permitted by Sections 107 and 108 of the United States Copyright Act without the permission of the copyright owners is unlawful. Printed in the United States of America.

10 9 8 7 6 5 4 3 2

Library of Congress Card Number: 00-107114

ISBN 1-57090-097-3 Trade Paper

ISBN 1-57090-118-X   Limited Edition Hardback

The author and publisher have made every effort in the preparation of this book to ensure the accuracy of the information. However, the information in this book is sold without warranty, either express or implied. Neither the author nor Alexander Books will be liable for any damages caused or alleged to be caused directly, indirectly, incidentally, or consequentially by the information in this book.

The opinions expressed in this book are solely those of the author and are not necessarily those of Alexander Books.

Trademarks: Names of products mentioned in this book known to be a, or suspected of being trademarks or service marks are capitalized. The usage of a trademark or service mark in this book should not be regarded as affecting the validity of any trademark or service mark.

Alexander Books™—a division of Creativity, Inc.—is a full–service publisher located at 65 Macedonia Road, Alexander NC 28701. Phone (828) 252–9515, Fax (704) 255–8719. For orders only: 1-800-472-0438. Visa and MasterCard accepted.

Alexander Books™ is distributed to the trade by Midpoint Trade Books, Inc., 27 West 20th Street, New York NY 10011, (212) 727-0190, (212) 727-0195 fax.

This book is also available on the internet in the **Publishers CyberMall.** Set your browser to http://www.abooks.com and enjoy the many fine values available there.

This book is dedicated to:

My wife Sally
She has been a balm to my uneasy existence during
the writing of this book.

I want to thank Opal for being such a faithful secretary.

Arlin and Rebecca did precious hours of editing
for which I am very grateful.

So many people have encouraged me over and over,
including members of my family.

I owe Ralph Roberts, my publisher, for suggesting several
times that I write my prisoner of war experience.

I'm sure we could say this book is a cooperative endeavor.

Buck Private T. Walter Middleton

CONTENTS

Foreword
by Ralph Roberts

More than fifty-five years have passed since the end of World War II; living veterans of this great conflict are now mostly in their 70s and 80s.

It is a war now older than most of us living, the guns long silent and still. I am not young, yet my birth was in December, 1945, just after the end of the war. But it is not–nor should it ever be– a war forgotten. Nor should the men and women who fought, who lived it, who won it, ever not receive the honor and recognition they will for all time deserve.

In the 1950s and 60s–as I grew from boy to man–World War II was readily a topic of conversation. I recall vividly sitting on our front porch on firefly-lit summer evenings listening to neighbors reminisce about the war. Those who had stayed behind–my mother, my dad (who had been too old to serve) told of the hardships, the shortages, the rationing. My father built tanks in Detroit during the war. My mother was one of those "Rosy the Riveter" ladies who built fighting airplanes– B29s are what she made.

Sitting on the steps, listening to the adults discuss the war remains vivid these more than forty years later. Mr. Webb on a hot summer's eve bringing live the chilling European winter in which he fought the Battle of the Bulge; Rex Hayes flying missions as a tail gunner in a B-17; my uncle Willis, a dental technician with a mobile hospital; Roger Williams, a painfully young infantryman in the lethal hedgerows after the D-Day landings; Chuck Hazelrigg doing combat construction on the Pacific islands as our forces island-hopped toward the Japanese heartland. Stories of sacrifice but, always, of victory.

The dark side of the war was only hinted at. There was the neighbor who drank a bit and, late at night, got out and fired his guns a lot. "His nerves were shot in the war," was whispered, but no one went beyond that.

Like many a young man from time immemorial, the reality of war I learned for myself the only way one can, by living through the horror underlying the glorious façade. As an infantryman in Vietnam, in the university of jungle combat, I graduated from novice to veteran with an understanding of the game of blood played out in wars.

As a writer, the dark side of the force, these untold, only hinted at sacrifices men and women make in war have revealed their true significance to me. It is, I think, even more in the realms of honor and glory to have suffered grievously for your country; to have been wounded seriously or have endured the unimaginable constant horror a prisoner of war undergoes. These are the greatest sacrificers, the *true* heroes, the men of steel behind bars of bamboo and iron.

Rex Hayes, back in the 1950s, did not tell me what happened after his B-17 was shot down, after he descended from the sunlight into years-long darkness as a German POW. But later he did give me a formal interview and I wrote with heartfelt emotion of his experiences in pain and squalor, in the cold German winters, in lack of food and the other hardships borne by prisoners of war in the European Theater.

I also interviewed and wrote the tear bringing story of Colonel Bob Bagley, prisoner of the North Vietnamese for seven years during the Vietnam conflict.

Yet, of all these great men (and they are great) there is no story so horrifying yet so inspirational as that of Walter Middleton. Walter was one of our brave soldiers in the Philippines who fought so bravely against hopeless odds against an overwhelming Japanese force.

"They were the first to fire and the last to lay down their arms and only reluctantly doing so after being given a direct order," said Lt. Gen. Jonathan M. Wainwright, the highest ranking officer to share their captivity.

Wainwright, Walter Middleton, and fellow soldiers were abandoned by MacArthur and his high command, left to surrender to the conquering forces. Walter survived the infamous Bataan Death March, only to be cast into the hell of Japanese prisoner of war camps in the Philippines and later in Manchuria.

The Bataan Death March was a forced march of 70,000 American and Filipino prisoners of war captured by the Japanese in the Philippines early in WWII.

Beginning at Mariveles, on the southern end of the Bataan Peninsula, on April 9, 1942, they were force-marched 55 miles to San Fernando, then taken by rail to Capas, from where they walked the final eight miles to Camp O'Donnell.

They were starved and mistreated, often kicked or beaten on their way, and many who fell were bayonetted. Only 54,000 reached the camp. 7,000 - 10,000 died on the way and the rest escaped into the jungle. And those that survived faced horrid years as prisoners of the Japanese.

It is a story of the dark side of war, but one from which comes light in the end.

I'll let Walter tell it to you now. It is his story.

Map drawn by T. Walter Middleton

Preface

For the benefit of those who might otherwise never know the early history of WW II, I am reaching back into my memory more than a half century and am trying to piece together facts as I recall them. Time has erased many of the details I could use now. Nature has been very kind and has dulled the sharpness of some painful experiences.

I feel a duty to share my experience in this book, but I dread the pain of reopening an old wound. Facts trying to find their way through a thousand flashbacks and nightmares like reruns of the most demonic atrocities known to man, can't be altogether without error. Fantasy has a way of invading reality in the imagination of an old soldier. I didn't want to tackle such an inhuman experience that is more than a half-century-old and relive it as I share it with you. But I must because of the absence of this information elsewhere.

Most of the printed material I have read concerning the Philippine Encounter has been books written by officers, heroes or professionals, some of whom were not there. These all had concepts taken from their own vantage points. Well and good.

But would you allow a buck private to share his perceptions from the bottom of the totem pole? Most of the soldiers were there, danger was the greatest and injuries more prevalent. Buck privates lie under the majority of white crosses in Asiatic cemeteries or lie alone on the battlefields. They were the most expendable.

Please remember this effort brings back reminders of too many horror scenes, massacres, places and times when Asian savages poured out their heathen wrath on unarmed American prisoners of War. Japanese War Lords created a hell on earth where literally thousands of our boys were butchered and starved to death during three and a half years of incarceration.

This particular portion of history was overshadowed by the Pearl Harbor atrocity that the media and politics used to raise an American explosion of war spirit and expansion. That is my honest opinion.

Not many details of the Philippine campaign got past Corregidor's propaganda machine bragging on the brave genius who had challenged the whole Japanese Armed Services. It was "General MacArthur did this" and "General MacArthur did that," hogging everything on the news going to America.

The nose to nose battles on Bataan were done by 24,000 American Soldiers and some great Filipino Scouts who held the Japs four months until America could arm Australia and thereby have a base of operation back toward Japan.

School books should at least state that the war started some place; that what we did those first four months changed the whole course of history in the Pacific. Perhaps someday some generous historian might discover Bataan and pen some benevolent and fitting comments for posterity. I wish.

After the war was over and General MacArthur had time to evaluate that first Bataan Campaign, the following quote is what he wrote:

> "Bataan with Corregidor—made possible all that happened since. History, I am sure, will record it as one of the decisive battles of the world. Its long protracted struggle enabled the Allies to gather their strength. Had it not held out, Australia would have fallen with incalculably disastrous results. Our triumphs today belong equally to that dead army.—It was destroyed due to its dreadful handicaps, but no army in history more fully accomplished its mission."

Appalachia Beginning

The Western North Carolina Mountains were a rather unique experience for a boy growing up. It was bittersweet but easy to get used to. Those hard depression years had lengthened more than half century of Civil War deprivation that lingered in the deep mountains far too long. We were the last place new concepts ever arrived.

Roads were "please don't rain" and very narrow. Cliffs and banks were tall and threatening. Curves were quick in and out of every little cove. Mountains and ridges were steep. Consequently, we were isolated even from each other.

People grew up and old without having enough money for even meager necessities at times. We were very poor and didn't know but little difference.

Enough food was grown in gardens and small acreage for family use. Hogs ran wild in some mountainous areas with family earmarks on them. Deer and other wildlife were available. Pork was the chief meat on tables. We had chickens when the preacher visited. Venison and small wild animals took up some slack. If a family had enough land they usually had pasture for a cow or two that furnished milk and milk products. Hard work was a must but we ate quite well. Those who managed best, lived best.

Mother used to pray that her children could break the old backwoods tradition and find a better life for themselves somewhere in the world. A mother's prayers and dreams must

At home in the Appalachian Mountains,
T. Walter Middleton and his dog.

have found grace somewhere. But answers don't always come today, I've found.

A one-roomed schoolhouse that doubled for a church was the busiest place in walking distance. My teacher father was a dedicated advocate of the three "R's" to the advantage of many mountain students. Money was so scarce part of the six-month school year he often had to teach without pay.

Sunday brought families close together for Christian fellowship and worship, the most meaningful event in a long week. Their sense of togetherness and their strong faith in God were a trusty support system. If their Sunday experience did nothing else worthwhile, they returned home smiling and feeling good inside. They could make another week now.

Besides school and work during my teenage years, my mountains gave me trails to hike, cliffs to climb and places to explore of rare scenic beauty. Miles and miles of trout streams were there for me. My choices were limitless and mine to make.

I became a rugged mountaineer with a built in endurance, which prepared me well for the difficult years ahead. Mountain memories gave me spiritual food during some lonely hours when Japanese imprisonment was at its worst.

2

Induction

"There's war in the air, you just watch and see," Mother told us. She said there was the same kind of fore talk people were hearing before W.W.I. Our radio was talking meaner and uglier constantly about military buildups and threats overseas in the European theatre. Out in town a large billboard had been hoisted up with "Uncle" pointing straight at me. Before we could get used to rumors and propaganda and scary talk everywhere we went, they hit us boys with an Ace Card, the draft.

People in town said the Draft Board was busy checking names and ages at the Register of Deeds Office. Before long I got a threatening like letter saying that I must needs register with the Draft Board under penalty of law. Mom was right, a mad war machine was being built for a war they hadn't started yet but one they intended to undertake soon. She had a distrust of our world leaders, which she backed up with some good reasoning. The way Mom saw it, we were going to have a big war to get factories in production and the economy booming. In the meantime they'd kill off most of the young men again and cripple lots of them. She gave me the creeps.

Someone got a wise idea that one way to beat the draft was to enlist for a year. I think they passed a law. Either way, "You're in the army now, you're not behind a plow." I didn't feel like there was an option. Juke boxes were belting out a

1939–T. Walter Middeton stands beside his prize 1938 Pontiac. It was about this time he started learning terms like 1A.

popular song, "I'll be back in a year little darling." Young fellows were guzzling more and more beer and quite a few of them getting engaged.

This was in the late thirties and President Roosevelt was bringing our country out of depression. Times were picking up some and more and more work was available. WPA and Civilian Conservation Corps along with a few others started giving people a little hope and some better clothes to wear. Moonshiners were hitting the jackpot.

About that time I got another one of those insulting, X-rated letters from the Draft Board saying I had been classified 1A and not to leave my present address without consulting them. That threw a kink into my long-range plans. It didn't do much for my short range ones either.

I decided against getting married. In a crisis of this dimension, there didn't seem to be much future in it. Then in only a few short months the Postal Service delivered another letter to my mailbox informing me that my number had been *drawn*. I was to report to the bus station in town no later than nine o'clock Monday morning next. I knew right then I'd been had. They had no respect for an individual. Why would there be a draft if someone wasn't about to start a war? Small comfort!

On Monday morning I kissed all the family and kinfolk I had on the mountain, some I didn't even know, and went to town which was about twenty miles away. About thirty of us had bunched up ready to leave Sylva, N.C. for parts unknown.

The town's number one lady told us in deep Southern how proud they were of us brave souls whose destiny it would be to save our Country from tyranny. She said they would be waiting with open arms and hearts to welcome us when we returned. What she didn't know was that she would die of old age before I made it back.

The United States Government transported loads of draftees hither and yon to several different Forts before they got who they wanted where they wanted them. They weren't to blame. They just weren't used to using old WWI leftovers and ways of doing things. I don't believe they'd figured out who was boss either.

I ended up in Fort Belvoir, Virginia Engineer Training Facility. They were organized. The old Engineer training was the hardest work I had done in my life. We trained for eighteen weeks on everything Combat Engineers would be asked to do. These included teaching individuals to take squads of Infantry or Marines and use them in emergencies such as building bridges or other on the spot crisis operations.

Out of that training Battalion about three hundred men were chosen to board a troop train going west via the southern route under secret orders. We reached San Francisco and were taken across the Bay to Angel Island where we joined A and B Companies of the 803rd Engineer Battalion.

Two things stand out in my mind as I look back. One was Alcatraz Prison that we passed going from Frisco to Angel Island. The second was the fact that I belonged to Uncle Sam 100%. Those men in prison weren't going anywhere. I didn't know where I was going but I'd be taking orders from Uncle.

Illustration from the Northwestern University Library's World War II Poster Collection

An Army recruiting poster from the late 1930s.

3

Organized

The 803rd Engineer Battalion was organized on Angel Island in the San Francisco Bay area. It consisted of three companies. Headquarters Company was the governing and planning group. They were in charge of all heavy earth moving equipment.

Graduate Engineers mostly staffed their outfit. Experienced operators and various specialists who were liberally rated came from Fort Leonard Wood, Missouri.

A and B Companies would be assigned projects, operators and needed equipment by Headquarters. Our main purpose was to build airfields in the Philippines but we were combat trained also.

B Company officials and staff as a skeleton structure was a product of Westover Field, Mass. They were already organized to the point where they would own and control every rating in B Company. Upon arrival this group was all chiefs and no Indians. But not to worry. Several hundred recruits were just in from Fort Belvoir, Virginia. They would beef up A and B Companies with commoners to do the routine labor without hope of advancement or ratings. We took a royal screwing from day one.

After my name made the B Company roster, everybody seemed congenial enough when we met and passed greetings but that was about as far as it went. Eventually we southern boys began feeling the heat from sarcastic remarks like, "cownpone," "mustard greens" or "How does yeall feel today?"

I knew I was different but I wouldn't have exchanged with them. My southern brogue made me obvious enough. Even the way I walked tagged me as a "Red Neck." Soon I was a "Damned Rebel" and other provoking anti-southern remarks. I had to deal with those people personally in my mountain way, one at a time. Before long word got around. It didn't take much of that stuff to be too much.

Lest I leave a wrong impression about my company's Yankee Staff, they were by no means all rascals. Two things they very obviously had. One was a family like alliance. They loosely stuck together. Second, they expressed varying degrees of a subtle spite against people living south of the Mason-Dixon Line. Most of them would readily admit it. As I think about it, that feeling about Yankees hadn't altogether died out down South either.

Socially and religiously we were at odds. I grew up somewhat isolated in the North Carolina Mountains and was deprived of the social contacts and relationships that city people had. We cared for each other and tried to live according to an unwritten code of mountain tradition that "everybody was somebody." Our religion was Independent Baptist, really independent.

My Yankee outfit was a composite of several nationalities who were mostly from cities and towns. They were street smart and experienced in most of the skills of coexistence. A majority of them were of Catholic background. So I found myself fitting into Uncle Sam's Army like a square peg in a round hole. At times, only my allegiance to America kept me in bounds. We did what we were sent there to do, but I walked a bastard road with a bad attitude.

4

Ship Ahoy

Rumors flew wild and fast over Angel Island; enough to keep us well confused about our destination. Headquarters Company equipment operators went over to San Francisco several days in a row loading their machinery aboard a ship.

Then our day came. We were boated over and put aboard the President Cleveland Liner. It had been luxurious in its day but that era had passed. Now converted into a troopship, the President Cleveland had lost its former glamour but was still useful to Uncle Sam. Sadly unaware of our destination we pulled out of port. We wouldn't know until we arrived, where we'd be.

We sang the customary, "Good-bye Ladies" to an empty dock. Then we sang, "Merrily we roll along" but it petered out before we were half through it. The huge Bay Bridge loomed above us like the door leading out of our world. Sure, many of us left our hearts inside hoping to retrieve them again sometime. Some did. Some didn't.

The smell of hot dogs was advertising our evening meal. We pigged out. There was more than plenty for everyone. No one left the galley hungry.

Shortly after the meal, misfortune hit us a double whammy. First, homesickness set in. Families had never felt this dear before. I had never really told them how much I loved them, not the way I should have. Now I am thousands of miles

The President Cleveland Liner, a former luxury liner converted to a troop carrier, passes under the Golden Gate Bridge.

away from home and just getting started. For the first time in my life I was homesick, bad homesick. I could hear others blowing their noses all around me. Anxiety was becoming common place.

Next, we hit choppy waters that got worse and worse. They could give this beautiful Pacific back to Balboa for all I cared. The ship wouldn't stay still. It kept dipping at the front, then the back, see-sawing, rolling, rocking and screeching all manners of sounds like a ghost movie. I kept my mouth shut. No need sharing how my heart or my guts felt with anyone. They had troubles of their own. Little spasms of nausea made me feel like a wimp. A He-man wouldn't succumb to such trivia.

One big fellow pushed and pulled and staggered by, mumbling that it was a hell of a way to start a voyage, homesick, a belly fully of wieners and the ocean going crazy. How right he was!

I lay on my stomach with my hands locked under my narrow hammock bed and rolled with the President Cleveland. Meanwhile, traffic got unusually thick up and down the aisles. Some fellows were moving fast toward what I heard someone call the "head." I began feeling a need to go so I started the short journey through the traffic. First I staggered one way then another, ran backwards into traffic coming my way. Before I found my balance I ran over one man three times, got side-swiped by another. Then I met some people I thought were going both ways at once.

As I stepped over a barrier at the door of the place, a knee-high wave of half chewed wieners was flung across the floor in every direction the ship rocked. I didn't want to go there as bad as I thought. The stench of hot dogs scrambled in stomach acid and other bodily waste was just too much to endure.

Up on deck was a sight of pity. Someone was hugging every post along the rail with both arms as if that was his guardian angel. Fishes had been religiously fed and quite a few prayers hadn't reached the amen part. Those poor soldiers looked pale green in the moonlight. Not one treasure in Davie Jones' Locker or Mermaid in his harem could have gained their attention that night. Between heaves they were confessing sins all the way back to childhood.

I found a place to hold on and peed into the briny deep, then returned down to my place and hugged my rope mattress till I slept a nap or two. I never got quite sick enough to upchuck. I didn't know why my clothes smelled sour.

It took three or more days for normal to set in. In time, men gradually started visiting the mess hall and going up on deck to see calmer more gentle ocean just being home to schools of flying fish that popped out of a wave and sailed a hundred yards or so. Porpoises made quick trips up to peep above surface.

Phosphorus trimming followed the edges of lazy little waves. Gulls made squeaks and squawks begging for hand-outs. The western sky captured my soul and body at sundown when I had free access to a Master Artist who spread, splashed, and blended miraculous pastels, tints, shades and tones all over the horizon, changing densities until the sun had long since gone down. A fabulous sunset left its lingering beauty up there till dark erased it.

I brought a little more faith and relaxation down with me when I retired that night.

A statue of a Hula Dancer in Oahu, Hawaii—the dancers were at the center of an Aloha encounter.

5

Aloha

Huge chains rattled as the anchor went down. There, right in front of us was a building with ALOHA way up on the front. Oahu, Hawaii had always been a dream place and suddenly, gosh, it still was! Out to our ship came the small boats with canned Hawaiian music setting the stage for our serenade. Did those grass skirted hula hips ever turn a shipload of soldiers on! How do they do that? A man can never forget his first ALOHA encounter.

Then we stood there on the rail feeling like a load of bums and watching the dignitaries and our officers boated ashore. Were those gyrating skirts for us or for them? Most of us took cold showers and sacked out early, more humble and wiser.

The next night out we were shocked to see our ship sailing completely "blacked out," no lights at all. That scared us. Other things we noticed made us apprehensive. When smoke showed up on the horizon, two "Tin Can" escorts that had just joined us would speed out there for inspection as if they were expecting trouble. I don't think they were just doing it for practice. There was no hint, not even a rumor on the grapevine that we might be in imminent danger, but we kept suspecting there was something we should know that was being kept classified.

I had heard somewhere back in my mountain raising about such a thing as foreboding, and I reasoned about whether or not it had anything to do with the dread and uneasiness inside of me. Listening to fellows talking for days,

President Roosevelt–1940

I learned that there was a general mistrust of our leadership and a worry about our future.

The following day on deck was pleasant and inviting. As it almost always happens, two army blankets had been spread twenty or so feet apart. Men knelt all around them praying to the God of Luck as the dice chuckled and rolled. I could almost feel their concentration as they talked to the dice, pleading for their number to come up.

I observed that those who played the longest accumulated the largest piles of cash. I noticed also that something about the manner they covered bets made it more business than luck. It didn't take but a few minutes for me to learn not to play. Luck just wasn't my thing.

Someone had a radio going sharing easy listening Hawaiian music. Something about the dreamy mood it created was fascinating. President Roosevelt broke in on the only station we could pick up. He bragged on the number of people listening to his "fireside chats," told how the economy was growing and started making some statements about war.

"I hate war," the President declared.

"My wife Eleanor hates war."

"My son John hates war." He continued. Someone in the crowd commented that everyone in the whole damned family must be peace loving. None of us were prepared for our President's next words.

"No draftee shall be taken out of the Continental limits of the United States unless in case of an attack." (Of course these are excerpts from his speech.)

A shipload of draftees went berserk. Many un-nice things were said about Mr. Roosevelt that people today would rate X, or maybe XX. To put it in plain language they "cussed" him for everything unholy. Solemn wishes that bordered on prayers, if answered, would heap many kinds of early demise upon him.

Soldiers with any horse sense at all knew the fuse was already lit for the big bang in the Pacific. We knew that Washington Brass weren't fooling anyone now but our folks back home. Good old trusting America. Oh! How she'd have to pay in tears, anxiety and sacrifice because of deceit going on in high places. We were a shipload of unwilling participants.

That old liner was just slow-poking along. I had no earthly idea how fast a vessel of this sort should travel but it definitely wasn't breaking any speed records and there was a war about to commence somewhere. Troops were pacing the deck till well past sack time. The sight of land would sure be welcome. One could at least dig a hole there.

Then again, perhaps we were over reacting, trying to cross the river before we reached it. I've often wondered why an officer or two of ours didn't drop around to chat a little occasionally. That would have helped and we needed all of the help we could get. Just maybe though they were feeling the same curse of the sea that we were? Or perhaps that would be fraternizing?

Corregidor an island in the mouth of Manila Bay.

6

Manila

The first time we knew for sure our destination, it was announced that we were entering Manila Bay. For hours we had been seeing land around us but actually we weren't sure of where we were. Bataan was on our left now and on its tip was a small town called Marevelles. Corregidor, on our right was an island five miles long and a mile wide lying directly in the mouth of Manila Bay, so they told me.

These places had no meaning yet to us. But one day they would be burned into our memory, branded there. It was dark when the President Cleveland docked in Manila. We soldiers would have been more than glad to ride him back home had orders been given.

Scores of busses just kept pushing in. As one moved out, another moved in siphoning up the line that was disembarking and whisking us into the dark city. Manila was totally blacked out and those bus drivers took us on one of the wildest speed runs in history. It was crazy, man. They absolutely took the wrong side of the street and stayed there except when they were screeching around the traffic, blowing their horns and dodging in and out amongst things we couldn't even see. I don't know how fast they let them drive in Manila, but they were getting by with murder. When our driver slammed on his brakes, they'd squeal and the bus would run sideways.

By the time the busload got to Clark Field we were prime candidates for the bug house. Soldiers who faintly knew how

Manila, a surprisingly large, fast-paced modern city.

to pray were fully prayed up and possibly there were a few converts.

The men at Clark Field mess hall welcomed us with three and four letter words they must have learned there in the Far East somewhere. If they were American, they were American far removed. Those men weren't happy about having to get up in the middle of the night. What could we expect? We got cold cuts and cold beans and a slice of stale bread to push with. That's what we got. I didn't say thank you because of their insulting attitudes. No one else did either.

The Air Force issued us those old WWI emergency cots and pointed toward Tent City. We wouldn't need blankets they told us. An old sergeant born just a little bit south of Maine said, "Goot noit yous guys."

Still black out, we rookies felt our way into those Army Rag Hotels and spent precious time trying to assemble beds with broken legs and missing parts. Learning to make do with what you have is half the battle, but some couldn't make do because one can't sleep on half a couch.

It couldn't have been much more than an hour of sleep before a bugle commenced an insulting noise outside. Those darned bugles can be a menace, don't you know? Briefing was mostly a dozen or so "don'ts" with a few "do's" mixed in. Two hours later, after the whole Air Force was fed and out, a hungry Engineer Battalion lined up and waited another hour before the mess hall grudgingly opened its doors to us.

A cook was crushing three eggs in each hand and squeezing them over a huge grill. You'd better like them the way he offered them to you. That cook was a yard wide, a yard thick and hairy as an ape. That wasn't a religious look on his face and it wasn't tolerating comments either. A few pieces of bacon were flipped out of a cold pile of pre-cooked side meat toward our plates. If it didn't land there, snatch it quick and keep moving to the toast pile. Two slices that could have been anywhere from black to white and a cup of what someone called coffee was what we sat down to. Boy, the Air Force really feeds good, we were told.

I think Fort Stotsenberg was an ancient military base before Clark Field was built nearby. Philippine Scouts and their families occupied a large part of the area and it furnished Air Force non-coms a place to shack up cheap. It was off limits to us Engineers, so a sign read. But we Engineers were learning fast about Army rules that were not enforced and spent a Sunday afternoon learning about liquid headaches in a bottle called A11A gin.

We had just spent some hours Saturday night at a wild life center called Angeles. There was "Anna's Moon-light Cabaret," "The Starlight Bar" and "Patty's Pom Pom Club", to name a few. Some nice fellows I think they called "MPs" took us back to camp.

Monday, over near the side of a parking area stood twenty or more of the most remarkable looking humans I had ever seen, displaying hand-craft of their own creating for sale. Most items at the wayside market were carved or made of bamboo and were easily packaged to ship home. The craft people were a tribe of "little people," three and a half to four feet tall. Filipinos called them "Negretoes" and said they lived a-top a mountain they pointed to a few miles away, in a colony.

Not being dressed well is the politest way I could say they wore only "G" strings. I wondered how those small helpless

looking ones might have survived the countless centuries behind them, what pre-history was like for them. I'd never heard
the "little people" story before and I was amazed.

B Company, 803rd Engineers soon moved out to a town
twenty or so miles away from Clark Field called Del Carmen.
A huge sugar plantation and a typical Mill complex was owned
by German immigrants and worked by Filipino labor. There we
would be building a large bomber base in the sugar field.

*A Negretoe man is shown beside a six-foot American in this
photograph from the 1910s.*

7

Del Carmen

D el Carmen was a nice, well kept little town on the outskirts of a three thousand-acre sugar plantation. Not far from town were sugar mills that provided employment for several hundred Filipinos.

Our camp was a half circle of old WWI tents several miles from town. Heavy earth moving equipment roared in every direction all day long clearing hundreds of acres of sugar cane where our huge bomber base began taking shape. A triangle of runways, each about five miles long, occupied the time of Co. B 803rd Engineers. We worked hard in torrid tropical heat.

Nights didn't cool much, but when one is tired enough, he sweats and sleeps. Come morning he is wet, sore and stiff. Water was stingily provided in lister bags that hung about over the camp area. It tasted strong with chemicals and was about as hot as most cafe coffee, not the kind of stuff one could get used to. Salt pills were close at hand where we ate, bowls full of them and we were constantly reminded about dehydration.

To prevent all work and no play our commander provided transportation for us to invade town one night a week. A pool hall, bowling alley, cinema and various other entertainment and loafing places furnished something for everyone. Some men nodded in the movies while others flirted with females. The sugar industry gave Del Carmen a higher living standard than any other town in the area. We intended to enjoy it.

Uniformed B Co. Engineers created new excitement in town but didn't necessarily raise moral standards. The female population grew. New shops opened. A tattoo parlor was needling the public. Business seemed to be picking up. Even small lads were out pimping for their sisters who were, "virgins Joe, two pesos only." (To them, a virgin was any woman who hadn't given birth.) Soldiers couldn't possibly ask for a more agreeable tropical paradise, but in only a few short weeks it would be paradise lost.

Down at a river that flowed right out of a large mountain range, we went each evening for a bath. There they were again, those "little people." The men were fishing with crossbow contraptions, which they used under water while their women did work on piles of bamboo. They were industrious little fellows.

We discovered they had some strange characteristics which answered questions we previously asked about their survival abilities. Their sight was keen with good night vision and their hearing superior to us Americans. The most surprising attribute was their ability to smell and track animals or humans. This alone made this midget race superior to other humans and at least equal to carnivorous animals. Filipinos said they would stay neutral in all conflicts. No doubt, all scouting parties could desire at least one in their ranks. What an asset their abilities would be out there in "no man's land"!

8

War!

The first Sunday morning in December, 1941 we Engineers awoke to a different bugle call. Company commander Ingersall explained that we had just heard "the call to arms." Japan had devastated Pearl Harbor along with our Pacific Navy.

Now, wasn't that a blow below the belt! Fear, anger, despair and a multitude of other emotions silenced a company of tough men. There was a sort of sick gut feeling inside me. Home had never seemed so far away. Hell had broken loose and we were right in the middle of the "bulls eye." America had only given us a one way trip and it opened up a new kind of trouble. I know how an animal feels when it is caught in an inescapable trap.

Tuesday Clark Field's Airmen flew in and parked their planes in a nice row, then went to the mess hall for lunch. A few minutes later Japan destroyed most of our Air Force there in a very few minutes. Nicholas Field was also struck, near Manila, with the same kind of destruction. The Japs had planned their strategy well. Lesser targets were taken in turn.

The day after Clark Field, as I remember it, we were bombed and strafed at Del Carmen. They practiced on us for weeks and used up a lot of ammunition. They knew we were preparing for American bombers. Those Japs weren't about to let that happen.

I spent my last thirteen dollars sending my family a telegram. I didn't want my parents worrying so much. I told them I was alive and I thought I had a fighting chance. One old timer told me thirteen dollars would buy a lot of bananas. I don't believe he had anybody back home.

In the short space of time that enemy planes weren't overhead, some of us were out salvaging fifty caliber machine guns from destroyed planes. A welder was building tripods for the machine guns. Ball and socket joints from the axles of GI (Government Issue) trucks which were also disabled, went on top of the tripods and gave the machine guns access in every direction. A couple or three of these mean machines with bicycle handles welded so as to maneuver them well gave the Japs an American surprise next invasion date. Two Jap planes were downed and some took 803rd bullets home with them, and it took the brave out of the lot of them. They became much more cautious. We received a presidential citation, which didn't help much.

Within an hour after Jap bombers riddled our runways with bombs, we were out there with dozers and other machinery filling the holes, patching the damage. That night Jap radio announced that they had destroyed enormous amounts of American property. Next morning their little photo planes couldn't find any damage at all. Sometimes repairing damage took us all night.

One day Tex, a slim young man with a slow Texas drawl was helping me service equipment working on a partially completed runway. We were Rebel Grease Monkeys doing our best to keep the outfit moving. Suddenly we became aware that all other heavy equipment had been shut down. Nothing was moving. When we looked up, approximately fifty bombers were coming in our direction. Our loaded truck was useless as far as speed was concerned in six to eight inches of loose dirt and dust underneath. Tex outran me to the sugar cane fifty or so yards away. I ran four or five rows into the field and flattened out. Suddenly another enemy attacked. I was prostrate on an anthill. Clad only in short pants and a pith helmet I made a tasty morsel for hundreds of those biting, stinging pests.

Bombs were strewn up the runway and one hit only forty yards away from us. Shrapnel was cutting sugar cane off just over our backs and ants were at work trying to disembowel and neuter me. Tell me this ain't war?

Dust almost smothered us. Ridding oneself of the present evil of those hungry monsters was priority number one, momentarily. A dense yellow smoke filled the air just after the bomb exploded parallel with us on the runway. If all of these things weren't enough, concussion from the bomb caused me to fill my pants. Sure, I was scared half to death but I don't think that was the cause. If you've been within forty yards of a thousand-pound bomb exploding, you'll understand.

I still hadn't checked on Tex. I yelled for him. I heard him mumbling something. I yelled louder. Then I saw him rise up in that yellow smoke. I saw his gas mask as he pulled it up. He said, "Middleton, do you smell anything?"

At a time like this a man's emotions are really keyed up high and anything can happen. At that moment I went into hysterics. It was the funniest moment of my life.

A half dozen tanker cars were parked in the vicinity of where we Engineers were surfacing a runway. The tankers contained sugar cane juice that made a fairly useable surface when mixed with soft dirt and was packed hard and tight, an Engineer innovation.

Fifteen or twenty Filipino workers took shelter under the tank cars just as the Jap planes came in on a strafing mission. The pilots evidently thought those tank cars were filled with fuel of some description so they made an extra pass or two over them. Nectar almost drowned the poor Filipino workers but, miraculously enough, none of them were hit by bullets. Those workers went in every direction and they never returned, having had enough war for a lifetime.

In the meantime, the Japanese were making ready to land at Lingayen Gulf. Our Air Force had only a half dozen aircraft to defend the shore and they did a good one-sided job. However, so few against so many was like a one-legged man at a tap dancing contest.

803rd got orders to move out. All equipment and supplies had to be loaded on trucks. Some heavy machinery was ambulatory and was sent on ahead. Small amounts of oil and grease that were out over the area needed to be retrieved. Tex and I went out after some lubricant we knew about. After loading our truck, we hit the dusty, partially complete runway and I was giving the old truck all it had, creating a terrible dust screen behind. Just as we entered a busy area I slowed down rather quickly so as not to hit anybody and a vehicle struck me in the rear. The driver first told a witness the dust blinded him, then started blaming me for quick stopping in his front.

I wanted it understood that I was not to blame but I didn't start a ruckus when I got out of my truck, just talked nice and easy.

"Don't be so damned innocent farm boy, yo po southern brogue won't get you anything but an ass whipping, you son of a bitch." I punched him.

I helped the fellow up and some one wiped the blood that was running from his face. I was flabbergasted. When I was a kid my grandpa had told me about the Civil War and that it was over. Sure, I was easy to spot as a southern boy but I thought people were created equal. Anyway, I stepped over and offered him my hand. He spat on it. I didn't help him up that time. I got in my truck and went about my business.

9

General MacArthur's War

Knowing that war was inevitable, General MacArthur centered his planes at and around Lingayen Gulf where he was almost certain Japan would make their initial landing on the Philippines. The General had cause to train approximately thirty thousand young Filipinos who had been conscripted into the service and were organized into Infantry, Artillery and other units as needed.

Philippine Scouts who were excellent, seasoned soldiers were stationed at strategic points where defense lines had been set up. The best leadership in the Island including General Wainwright led each unit and knew the battle plans well.

War ships bombarded the Gulf for a week or more before the Japanese Imperial Army landed on December 22 or 23rd. General Homma with the elite, well trained, well-equipped invaders spearheaded into General MacArthur's forces. The Japanese had a much superior fire power against our antiquated WWI equipment. Causalities were high among the entrenched Filipino rookies. They panicked and, terror stricken, fled by the thousands down the mountain range that reached south through the center of Bataan. One observer stated that those mountains looked like anthills crawling with deserters.

General MacArthur was receiving reports, negative reports, of his prized defensive outfits while he paced Malinta Tunnel in a rage. He didn't leave Corregidor, but orders to regroup and retreat toward Bataan went out to his beleaguered soldiers. The

General MacAuthur on Corregidor.

General's big plan had exploded, although General Wainwright and his Filipino Scouts fought delaying tactics on their withdrawal south through the central plains and received favorable commendations. Some of the other officers caught MacArthur's wrath and were demoted. Dugout-Doug's ego was deflated, quite somewhat!

Most of this information was passed around from group to group. Our officers were kept abreast of all current news and each outfit began to be coordinated toward places and jobs according to their abilities.

The Japs landed about December 23rd and B Co. 803rd moved out from Del Carmen the 26th. Roughly guessing, we were about sixty miles apart. But we at Del Carmen had been bombed and strafed since December 8th or 9th. We knew what that kind of war was like from the beginning. It was a shame to leave such a great potential Bomber Base for the Japs, but there were other airfields to be built, roads to keep in repair, and battles to fight down the Bataan Peninsula. It was becoming obvious that would become our last stand.

10

Orange 3

Orange 3 was an overall plan that had been put together by high ranking brass pertaining to the defense of Luzon before war with Japan was imminent. I'm not sure that General MacArthur's "dream team" was a part of Orange 3. Nor was it as well-planned and prepared, as long-range plans should have been.

When Japanese troops landed at Lingayen Gulf, General Mac's army came apart like a split sack of beans. General Wainwright, General Parker and other responsible officers, took the Filipino scouts and what they had left, organized and fought delaying action south through the central plains. That part could have been Orange 3.

On or before Christmas the plans started coordinating movement toward Bataan. There was very little panic and each outfit was given orders when to go and what to do. Commanding officers were responsible for exact obedience so Orange 3 might do its clockwork and get every outfit down Bataan to where it should be.

803rd B Co. was to stop at the upper tip of Bataan and build an airfield near a town called Hermosa, hoping and praying that America would send planes. We were to keep the roads to the north open until every outfit was through.

On our way toward Bataan we stopped at a small white school house and ate our Christmas dinner a day late.

When we arrived at Hermosa, surveyors were beginning their work. Some men were getting equipment and supplies organized and in place. A dozen or more shacks stood along out through the area where the airfield would reach. Three of us were detailed to go and see if anyone might still be occupying those places and if so, bring them out.

I wasn't expecting what I walked in to at one of those shanties. A young Filipino woman lived alone there.

"My husband go to war, I wait here for him. We marry short while ago only. I desire for him very much." Each time the poor thing explained how lonely she was, her long, loose gown like dress was loosing its straps from her shoulder.

She saw me look at a large banana lying on a stool. As she stepped out of her dress that had fallen to the floor, she offered me "banana for love." My stomach and conscience collided but only for a moment. Nervously I reached out and touched her.

We divided the banana and I directed her to a truck with others going to the Civilian Compound on lower Bataan.

The road from Manila came up and circled by Hermosa down Bataan. For over a week traffic from Manila kept the roads loaded to capacity day and night. Every vehicle was full and had passengers hanging on everywhere one could find a handhold. Bataan was the place to go. Quite often GI trucks carried loads of service men who had been serving in the Manila area.

A few days after Christmas, General MacArthur declared Manila an open City. In the meantime, we at Hermosa watched outfits pass us toward Bataan. Each outfit came by us one after another in a very orderly way. Only one or two seemed in too big of a hurry. One of the first was Clark Field Air Force and then others. The last was a part of General MacArthur's "Dream Team." Philippine Scouts were most dependable as soldiers. I'd hate to tangle with that group of soldiers. They gave the appearance of the best I'd ever seen, and such was their reputation.

The Japs great leader General Homma, and his forces entered Manila about New Year's Day and sacked the town.

Carr Hooper and his wife were among the civilian prisoners in Manila. They were my friends even before the war. We had

Fifty years later, the scars of the Japanese guns can still be seen.

been neighbors. We were often together after the war was over and we were back home. Carr confided to me the extent of General Homma's influence in Manila. Women and things of monetary value were first choices, and then trinkets. He blew the city up; tried out all of his guns on all buildings. Possibly some are still pockmarked from that celebration.

Just as our airfield was finished at Hermosa we got orders to move. Two weeks had passed. Two tanks came and followed us down. They told us the Japs were just a matter of hours behind. That would have been General Homma heading for Manila.

Hermosa Air Field would belong to the Japs now. We built it in good faith believing that America would come. Broadcasts from over on the rock (Corregidor) kept encouraging us with promises that it would only be a matter of time until hundreds of planes and ships, thousands of fresh soldiers and supplies would arrive.

In the meantime, Japs had started bombing towns and bridges down Bataan Peninsula before beginning their offensive, which they expected to finish within a month or less, so we were told.

Fortification built to slow the advance of the Japanese.

B Co. 803rd had orders to build another airfield at Pilar. We had several miles of road to keep open so supplies could easily reach the Orange 3 front lines of defense, not yet active.

In a jungle across the road from Balanga, then the next little town beyond Hermosa, we found a good enough bivouac area. We dug straddle trenches a-plenty zigzagged across one end of the compound. A waste water hole was excavated underneath our water trailer. Other work was done, as it seemed necessary. Care was taken to keep our road into camp camouflaged and our old beat up cots in as comfortable a place as possible. It was about all the home a soldier could ask for in such a jungle.

The bright moonlight made it easy to work nights, but sleeping in the jungle days got hot and uncomfortable. Mosquitoes had a feast. One day we were aroused by planes overhead. We knew the sound. Japanese dive-bombers began tearing the little town apart. Almost all of the people had evacuated. There are always some hard cases that have to be shown.

All of a sudden, we realized we had neglected to dig foxholes for ourselves. I made a run for the straddle trench but it was already level full of early birds. I thought of the waste water hole under the water trailer. It was full as well but I made a place for myself anyway. I'd heard that a good soldier never came up short. The greasy water where all meskits had been washed after meals, had soured but it floated off down the hill having been replaced by four men.

Only a minute or two later a bomb hit our camping area. Shrapnel went through our water tank and water started running down over us four men. The bottom man had greasy mud in his eyes and was crying that someone was bleeding to death. It was really a scary few moments. I didn't hear anyone screaming hurt. Planes had finished their job and were gone.

We climbed out of our pits. No one was hurt, but the bottom layer of men coming out of the straddle trench was ready for a bath and our water trailer was empty.

I heard someone screaming down where the little town had been and trotted down there. A Filipino old lady sat on the ground wailing and pointed to a house that was almost demolished. I crawled in but was hindered by crushed debris. Finally I found a little six or seven year old girl that shrapnel had cut almost half in two. Ten or fifteen minutes later I had her free and carried her out to the elderly lady and laid the child in her arms. I stood by her and grieved with her for a short while. This was one of several moving yet somewhat similar experiences we were involved in from time to time. Usually when we think of war, it involves only Armed Services Personnel. But please, will you remember the innocent women and children affected in all armed conflict.

President Roosevelt signing the official Declaration of War.

Abucay Hacienda

Big Freddy was one of the 31st Infantry boys, country as cornbread. He told me they were set up and ready for the Japs. We talked about it in O'Donnell Prison Camp later and Freddy said the Japs just sauntered into a trap like a group of school kids going home after school. He was under the impression that there were two or three companies that the 75-mm guns zeroed in on and almost wasted the lot of them in one pile. A few got back into a sugar cane field and must have been joined by some late comers. They attacked again that night and got tangled up in old W.W.I barbed wire stretched in rolls all across the front line. Our infantry machine guns thinned them out. That was the first hand to hand fighting on Bataan.

At the end of two weeks our men were having to wear their gas masks because of so many decomposing bodies out front. The heat and stench was unbearable. Japan took a beating.

The Abucay line extended from Manila Bay to the foot of a large mountain that the map called Mt. Natib, about half way across Bataan. From the western side of the mountain to the ocean General Wainwright controlled the line with his Filipino Scouts. Everybody thought Mt. Natib was impenetrable and didn't bother to set any defense there.

The Japs found this thick jungle deserted and, from somewhere, obtained Filipino sugar cane machetes enough to carve a path across Mt. Natib. I've heard that some wandering Filipinos tipped General Wainwright's men off about the Japs and gave them time to retreat before the Japs. He possibly engaged the Japs a few times to slow them down in order for the Americans on the Abucay side of Mt. Natib to retreat also. There were 2 weeks of intense fighting then the Americans retreated. I'm sure the Japs were surprised at our resistence.

General MacArthur's fame had spread far and wide. America was giving him credit for his heroic resistance against such a formidable foe. There was no publicity at all that American forces had been placed on half rations a week before they fired the first shot on Bataan. Twice more our daily ration was cut in half. Let it be known here and now, Japan did not defeat our American forces on Bataan. General MacArthur did. He had made no provisions for extra food and medicine when he began asking for various army units from America. Some sources tell of large caches of supplies. But if there were any they were mostly on Corregidor. Those Corregidor defenders didn't have to make a "Death March" nor did they look deprived of food, to me they didn't. Believe me, Bataan had been hungry since before a Jap set foot there.

I have wondered why General MacArthur didn't share the tons and tons of food that some men knew he had on Corregidor.

December 7, 1941 –May 6, 1942

This ship, The "Bataan" [LHD5], is dedicated to those valiant American Forces that, at the beginning of WW II, fought a gallant five month battle defending the Philippine Islands against the well equipped and adequately supplied Imperial Japanese Forces.

The defenders were ultimately forced to surrender, not for lack of courage, valor nor the inclination to continue. Their defeat was directly attributable to America's failure to initially provide them the essential equipment and supplies required to accomplish their assigned mission, along with the Nations' inability to reinforce and resupply the besieged defenders during their first five month period of combat.

Vol. 52 Quan November, 1997

(Part of the inscription on a plaque aboard the "USS Bataan".)

12

Backing Up the Troops

After finishing the Pilar Air Field the 803rd was busy keeping the roads open, doing guard duty at vulnerable places along the shore line and being there when general crises arose.

We had moved to Kilometer 169, which was five miles up the mountain above Mareveles. Mareveles had principally been a Navy town and the primary employment was at the Navy Base down at the end of town.

Some of the natives made their living from the ocean. Their strange little sailboats, which they used for fishing and crabbing, were anchored all along the shore. The USS Canopis occupied a nook out in front of the Naval Base. Not too far away an old "Flying Coffin" sea plane swung and wafted around its anchor, constantly riding the little waves.

The Japs couldn't have been proud of their marksmanship. Dozens of times dive bombers zeroed in on the plane and reported it sunk but when their little camera plane came around it always carried back pictures of the "Flying Coffin" still moving about down there as the waves determined.

The 803rd Engineers built an air field the long way across Mareveles. Working hard and sweating, dodging bombs and strafing seemed to be a part of each dreadful day. Inhabitants evacuated town and took up residence in the jungle although I do believe the little sail boats were out at night. A

few times the Japs strafed their boats around the shore line.
The boat men patched them up.

Most of the town was close to the base of the mountain and
the airport didn't damage them a great deal except by
bringing the Jap planes overhead. I remember a large church
that was about the center of town. Just seeing the steeple
evoked many prayers by people who passed. A large brick
oven was then cold and useless but a reminder of better
times when they had bread to eat.

Japs had been coming down the west coast of Bataan and
making landings. Our road up the west coast of Bataan toward
Bagac was in a terrible state of disrepair. In order for our forces
to defend our west coast, we moved equipment and rebuilt
most of the road. All the time Jap planes were sniping away at
us, keeping us watchful and uneasy. They had been practicing
on us ever since Pearl Harbor. Jap planes had always paid the
Engineers more than enough attention.

Two miles above the airfield the Japs blew a bridge. Because
of a possible threat, we were dozing a ford around the blown
bridge during daylight hours shortly after it was bombed. Three
GI rag-topped limousines came down the road. We didn't
know when they went up. They didn't know the danger they
were in, but they were flying a General Flag and should have
had better sense.

They seemed anxious to detour the blown bridge but we
weren't more than half through the dozing work. The soldier
who was standing out watching the sky for planes told the big
brass it would be thirty more minutes. They weren't happy and
told the soldier so.

The young watchman informed them that there was a
little spy plane buzzing around overhead and he could have
other planes there in a matter of minutes. He told them, "If
I wanted to save my ass I'd get back up there in the jungle till
these fellows finish. They're working as fast as they can."
They went.

Next day we heard that General MacArthur and his staff
had toured the troops on Bataan the previous day. Strange
they would pick an area where it was practically deserted and

Pontoon bridges were used to bypass bombed out bridges.

not visit even the makeshift hospitals where it might have made a difference.

Again, General MacArthur might not have felt comfortable confronting all the hungry troops. But America heard about his visit to Bataan that evening. Corregidor made it a point to tell the folks back home about the General and his fearlessness.

Not more than a mile from Mareveles, as the crow flies, the Japs landed a group of their Marines on Bataan. Part of the 803rd Engineers went down and embattled them for a week and then a Filipino Scout outfit finished the job. Those Scouts were more than matches for Japanese Marines.

My job was the "grease monkey" to the heavy equipment. My boss who kept a record of which equipment was serviced when, was a Corporal. The truck driver was a Corporal. I was a buck private and rode in the cab of the truck with them. All I had to do was change the oil in each piece of heavy equipment that was operating and use the grease gun at every lubricating fitting. I just had to crawl under each dozer, take the bolts out of the dust pan opening and drain old oil, replace everything and refill the motor with the right amount of oil. After this operation I had to fill each piece of equipment with Diesel fuel and load my lube equipment back on the truck. The two Corporals were waiting for me in the cab of the truck. Do you see why I appreciated my good Yank friends? Well, they did watch for enemy aircraft, I didn't mention that.

For a while I had a Filipino teenager as an aid. He stood close to the cab on the back. As we drove up the runway one day my Filipino began beating on the cab. We stopped. He was excited and said he suspected one of about a dozen men going toward their boats. We turned and drove back. Sure enough, a Jap Marine had taken clothes from some Filipino civilian and was trying to make his way back to the Jap front lines. We identified him easy enough. He didn't make it.

13

The Orion — Bagac Line

After two weeks of extremely fierce fighting at the Abucay line, our troops were withdrawn to another previously planned position. They were forced to abandon their first line of defense at Abucay but the cost to the Japanese was expensive indeed. If we had been given plenty of food and medical supplies, we just might have whipped those bastards. Huh!

A rough, stony road crossed Bataan from (as I remember it) Pilar on the Manila Bay side to Bagac on the China Sea side of the peninsula. The American and Philippine soldiers dug in their line with that old road behind them. Combat units and provisions could readily be moved on that road to any place of need on the line, unobserved by the enemy. The old road was in need of repair. Engineers worked it out and cut some connecting lanes up to the trenches.

Another mountain came into use but this time in America's favor. Mt. Somat that stood about the middle of the American line was a dormant volcanic shell of a mountain. The top was huge and hollow with some smaller foliage growing around its lips. Filipinos called it the "Dragon's Nest." Unattached soldiers of Philippine origin were persuaded to backpack supplies such as were available, up to the summit and make ready for another Japanese attack.

January had been a tremendously eventful month for Bataan's defense. Now, the last phase was about to commence.

Two months of nose to nose fighting, grit and brawn and brains was ahead.

Besides the hard fighting on the front line, Japan struck in about three places south of Bagac, making landings on Bataan from the China Sea. That called for every outfit that was not on the front line to make ready and go to those landing zones in a hurry. Japan got her tail whipped at all three places. Most of those were untrained in infantry fighting but they did themselves proud. Anybody can fight when they have to.

By the end of February the intense fighting on the Orion – Bagac line had slowed down considerably. Japan had been the big loser in combat up to now. Our lines had been pre-picked and everything to our advantage worked out by Orange 3 planners. Rumors were that Japs were having problems the same as we were. They were battle fatigued, hungry and disease was taking them out fast. Both sides were suffering from shortages of essentials. By this time it took grit and grace for a man to stagger up to the front lines. Sure, we loved our country but we had our backs against the sea and we couldn't go anywhere.

We had lost General MacArthur from Corregidor. He had escaped to Australia and left General Wainwright in charge. Someone said the General made a declaration after he reached Australia, "I shall return!" I've heard an old saying, "good riddance to bad rubbish." I thought it applied there. Scores of the guys had some old fashioned "cussin" going about it. His neglect had harmed an army. He left Bataan ready for the kill, starved to death and deserted.

Even though we Engineers were busy working at every task needed behind the battle lines, we were combat trained and were always ready to discontinue whatever we were engaged in and fill a vacancy at any point the Japs made a landing or applied heavy pressure. Our specialty was airfields but the Japs had a habit of blowing bridges and bombing roads. They blew towns to smithereens, blocking traffic for hours and dive-bombed the traffic; dive-bombed us as we were trying to get what was left of the town out of the road.

Those little tattletale planes were overhead most of the day directing Jap bombardment. They were systematically making

Engineers working on a bridge.

a total wreck out of Bataan. We couldn't build bridges one day and get them blown to kingdom come the next, so we built fords around the destroyed ones. Much of our work was done at night, as much as possible.

When one little town was destroyed, people in the next one down would leave for cover out in old roadways where there was thick timber or in a jungle. They were hungry and scared just as we were.

I thought about what it would be like back home if this kind of warfare was going on. Would they throw up lines of defense and fight like hell right on and on like we were doing until they were sick and starving and desperate, almost as if eternal life depended on it? God forbid! That was what we were laying our lives on the line every minute for, to keep America free. We were just making the first down payment on it. For the rest of our lives we'd still be paying no matter how long that would be.

No one knew how important each day, each hour was; we had no way to know that the whole Pacific War to come was balanced on sheer will belonging to us and us half dead. America doesn't know how close the whole Pacific Theatre

It don't look like much, but it was "our" road. Working mostly at night, the Engineering Unit worked hard to keep the roads open.

came to belonging to the Japs. If we'd caved in a week earlier, America likely wouldn't have reached Australia in time.

During the slack period in March things were going on behind the lines. General Wainwright was utilizing every truck, tank, half-track or any piece of equipment that might be needed in any way. He was mobilizing at least two infantry units that might be rushed anywhere the Japs exerted unusual pressure. That old rough, rocky road featured well into the best use of all we had left. We knew the Japs were not idle. Just stick your helmet up a little on your bayonet. They were still there. New recruits and firepower would soon attempt to get revenge for four months of stubborn defense.

Shortly after the first of April, the second or third I think, the Japs started shelling our line with a terrible barrage of large shells that lasted all day. The next day was the same except they also bombed us.

A fresh Jap Infantry outfit began driving into our line. One mistake they made was that, they tried breaking through at Mt. Somat. The old mountain belched fire again, this time with machine gun fire. Did the Japs ever pay at the Dragon's Nest! But the large fresh Jap forces were just too much for the sick and exhausted American soldiers, and on April fifth our lines began to crumble. The next day our Bataan defenders made a gallant counter-attack to gain back their old line but we lost a face to face, nose to nose battle and General Wainwright's "battling bastards of Bataan" were no match. We had to retreat. General MacArthur had left orders with General Wainwright to fight to the last man. General Wainwright disobeyed that order and was not forgiven until the war was over.

At this point, the handwriting on the wall was evident. We had been double-crossed by those we had trusted. We had to believe in America but our hearts were broken.

For months word had been coming from Corregidor encouraging us to fight on and on, that help was on its way. They mentioned ships by the score, hundreds of planes and thousands of troops. Over and over they told us this. But the weaker and more exhausted we became the more they cut our food. There was something very contradictory here that we'd been seeing for some time and we didn't want to believe.

Each evening Tokyo Rose did her thing on the radio. According to her, no help was coming, America was just plain out lying to us. She brought little doubts into our minds, reasoned with us, debated. Oh, Rosie had a winning way about her. She

Barbed wire was part of the fortifications that helped slow the Japs down.

reminded us Japan had demolished our Pacific Fleet and no way could the United States have put another fleet together that would survive the Japanese blockades. She had some very attractive propaganda and chided us with sexual hints.

Now we had next to no food at all. We had lost fifteen to twenty pounds and were hungrier than ever. Diseases were rampant and forty percent of our fighting men out sick. We had two large makeshift hospitals near Cabcaben with scarcely any medicine to treat sick and wounded men.

Those of us on the front lines were no match for fresh Japanese recruits with superior weapons and no shortage of ammunition. I heard several men say they were saving one cartridge in their old 30.06 WWI Springfield. The war on Bataan was all but over. Yes, we had been double-crossed. Hope was gone. Our own country had deserted us. Most of us felt we had lost the war and lost our country. I wonder why there was no one to tell the people in America what a shabby ending had come to their boys on Bataan? My father told me when I returned home after the war that American people had no knowledge whatever that their boys were being double-crossed and deserted or that their families were being misled and lied to.

14

Kilometer 169

Kilometer 169 was just at the top of Bataan Mountain where it began to level out. Mareveles was about five miles down at the bottom of the mountain. We had been bivouaced in the Jungle there for several weeks and had worked out from there on road projects and on Mareveles airfield. Japs were continually bombing out bridges and at night we would build fords around them. During the day part of my outfit was out foraging for food, just anything edible. One day I killed a small wild game chicken and boiled it in an old water bucket out in the jungle. I didn't want company.

They thinned the monkeys out pretty well and I kept my pet named "Chongo" on his leash in camp. He was my closest friend I guess and I don't think anyone was hungry enough to touch him. We had some close calls together and he seemed to realize when we were in trouble. But I had to take him down to the civilian refugees' compound and give him to the most kind-hearted-looking person I saw. Chongo and I both cried good bye and he clung to me. I turned and walked away fast. But my outfit was going to the front. We knew we weren't going to be backed up by able bodied, experienced infantrymen this time. As tired, sick and hungry as we were, one spot up there was ours to defend and we were ordered to go. Most of us went but some stayed at camp.

All of B Co. 803rd was not on the front. Our first sergeant got sick with yellow fever up the back and the poor man's nerves just about cried him to death. I don't know how many had to stay with him and support him in his panic attack. Some did. Others were obligated to stay in camp and destroy records, equipment and God only knows what else.

A Captain Thomas from Headquarters Co. led us to the front as our commander. He was promoted to Major that day. I don't know what happened to our Company commander. Of course some officers and company non-com's aren't expected to do front line duty. The majority of us commoners didn't feel welcome around our headquarters tents. We scarcely knew our officer personnel. We had no idea what their duties were, when during these crisis days, there was no company business to keep them busy. A corporal from Ohio was promoted to First Sergeant to replace the one that lost his nerve and proudly did his job. I understand several of the men who stayed in camp, even the cook got decorated for their service over and above their ordinary duty. None of these things were ever hinted about after the war was over at conventions. There's such a thing as shame you know.

The Japs had been quieter than usual all day. A burst of gunfire opened occasionally. Knee mortars were lobbed over in our vicinity every thirty minutes or so. No pattern just nerve busters and shrapnel scattered in every direction. That'd make a man dig, believe me, and shoot when he could.

An outfit now gone, deserted the battle line and had left a man with shrapnel in his back lying near my position. He was breathing and moaning. That was all one could tell about him. I dropped water into his mouth when I could. Evidently his buddies were in too big a hurry to take him along. In my opinion that is much too big of a hurry.

We were worried about the line to our left where the wounded man's outfit should have been. Our scouts came back with news that the line was deserted for at least a half mile. That said the Japs were just anywhere they wanted to be and it was after sundown. Word was passed around that we would make an orderly pull out just after dusk and return to our trucks which were less than a mile away. None was willing to help me get the wounded man out.

With a blanket I found, and two bamboo poles, I tried to fashion a drag sled to get the wounded man out. None of my outfit seemed inclined to give me a hand but I was determined. They passed me by and went out of sight into a banana grove at the bottom of a long hill they would climb toward the trucks. Two Filipinos had come by and promised to help me but in a short time they sneaked off into the dark. Every time my drag sled bounced, my soldier moaned loud, almost hollered.

I hadn't gone another fifty yards when four or more rifles opened up on us. They could tell our position by his moans. Every time I moved him he made a strange painful noise and those guns would fire. One bullet hit him and killed him instantly. One came through a banana tree and hit me in the buttock. I went down stunned for a few moments and then scrambled to my knees. I shot at a muzzle flash and got a scream of pain. I must have gotten him. I knew I had to move the way my outfit went. It was a painful climb up the ridge.

As I reached the top our trucks were moving out. I was staggering along using my rifle as a crutch. I barely made the last truck. No one seemed to be alarmed much that I was wounded and bleeding. I guess they just weren't paying attention. Our battle for Bataan was over.

Returning down the same old roadway we had come up before, our convoy got a rare view of the final battle on Bataan. A small plane hardly anyone knew we had, came up Manila Bay. Not more than a mile away it dropped two-parachute flares that lit the whole bay area. A number of Jap landing barges, were coming in for an invasion of lower Bataan. Not a gun fired until they had all come ashore. Suddenly the whole earth seemed to quake and explode from gunfire in the most terrible battle we had ever witnessed. Five minutes and it was over except a few short bursts.

By the time our convoy reached the battle zone hundreds of Japanese bodies were being moved out of the road. We looked up on the other side of the road from the landing and there in the tropical moonlight set a half circle of every able tank and half track on Bataan. They had waited until the landing was all complete then opened up with a surprise ambush that wiped the Japanese out and piled up the most dead bodies we had seen at one place. I'd estimate four to six hundred Japs had taken a blood bath at this spot after our lines were hopelessly collapsed. Some Jap commander had used bad judgment and lost his men in useless bloodshed after the war was over on Bataan.

General Wainwright broadcasting the order for all American units to lay-down their weapons.

15

Company B's Last Night Together

B Co. 803rd got back into bivouac about 11:00 P.M. on April 7, 1942. We were exhausted. I caught a little water in my helmet and cleaned up my right buttock and leg. I had kept a clean pair of dungarees and a pair of shoes which came in handy at this time. Someone poured my bullet hole full of iodine and patched it up good. I guess we all sat around and thought. I hurt. Of course I'd get the last bullet at the front lines and have to learn to live with it.

No one slept. We were not ashamed of the efforts we had made, the battles we had fought. I guess the only shame I could accept was my part of the shame my country had brought upon herself, the disgrace of deserting her fighting men without food, medicine or supplies of any kind and expecting them to make America proud. Little wonder we were overcome by a savage, unmerciful foe. Promises! Over and over vain promises. That had kept us fighting, not on energy but guts alone. We were blaming everyone we could think of that might have hurt us.

Oh, yes, they promised us over and over, more than enough to do the job and we were foolish enough to believe. If one couldn't trust America, who could be trusted? The longer we fought and starved the more hope went down the drain. We were disillusioned, in despair and were lashing out. We had plenty of time that night to let it all brand itself into our souls, waiting for a Godforsaken tomorrow that left us dead inside, sick outside. I had eaten one third of a can of

Spam in twenty-four hours but hunger wasn't my greatest problem. Now it was over. We had done all we could do. No help came.

What can you say to a band of men, Americans, who had given their all and were waiting for the enemy to come in and take them officially? Our officers said they were just as afraid as we were. That wasn't too much of a revelation. For all of us, disappointment of this magnitude was almost too great to bear.

It was coming daylight. That sick feeling got a little worse. I'm sure we were all trying to get hold of something that would give us courage enough to take this blind step into the future. We were men without any hope, too grieved to cry.

Just after daylight they came, came into our bivouac area. Slowly, irregularly dispersed, guns at ready. We were face to face with the Imperial Nipponese War Machine. We were no more threat to them but were their "much hated Amelican enemy."

Several of us learned what the business end of a bayonet felt like before those Japs got us on the road down toward Mareveles. That would be the assembly ground. I wonder if some people are just naturally bred and born savages? We were very angry men; angry at the Japs, angry at our country's leaders. We could never be the same again. Never. We were men without a country, Battling Bastards of Bataan; No Pappy, No Mammy, No Uncle Sammy.

I believe they say about ninety thousand American and Filipino prisoners were taken on Bataan. Before they were free again, more than half of them would be dead.

16

The Bataan March of Death

Japanese soldiers herded thousands of American Prisoners of War onto the Mareveles Airfield. Victory happy savages screeched out orders that we had no way on earth to know the meaning of. We had lost control and with it had to a great extent lost identity. All we were at that time was prisoners and we didn't know what that meant.

When Jap guards began jabbing men with bayonets and pointing up the road, we understood what that meant. We began falling in line and marching. Our formation was about eight to ten men wide in a open rank line. Jap drovers hustled along each side at about twenty to thirty-yard intervals urging us on faster.

In the five-mile climb to the top of the plateau we tasted some of what was ahead. Our bodies were already hurting. Some were exhausted, so out of shape they began vomiting and others having complications they didn't understand. One man I saw was having chest pains.

Two and a half months of listening to and fighting for a lying General without one square meal a day had made us helpless creatures in the hands of a nation that had murdered without mercy millions of Chinese people. What good could we expect?

More than a hundred thousand American and Filipino people had been deceitfully used and premeditatedly left without a snowball's chance in hell to survive. We were now beginning a sentence that had deliberately been passed upon us without an explanation or an apology. At this point I think I could have spoken for every prisoner on that road. We were angry and afraid. Angry at the man most responsible for dumping us into another life and death crisis. We were afraid of the uncertainty of our future.

The Bataan March of Death led up the Manila Bay side of Bataan Peninsula where most of the little towns were located. The road was hardtop and was hot enough to fry a steak on. Fear of what lay ahead disturbed us most as discomfort grew.

We didn't know that the Japs were using us prisoners to shield their artillery from Corregidor's big mortars. I guess they didn't expect Corregidor to retaliate. We could hear their heavy guns firing just ahead, evidently giving the Rock (Corregidor) a pounding. We were in sight of Cabcabin Air Field which we Engineers had built a month earlier.

One of the "Big Guns" on Corregidor.

Suddenly we sensed that huge mortar shriek in just over us and we were flat on the road in a heart beat just as it exploded. I saw a beautiful sight I shall cherish as long as I live. That Jap artillery piece went up exchanging ends and rolling about fifty feet in the air. Men and debris were up there among the dust and smoke. Today it is very vivid in my memory, not unlike a camera shot.

We Americans rejoiced silently that a small portion of America was zeroed in on our enemy and some service man pulled the trigger. I must have relived that scene a hundred times, always when I needed a little extra strength to keep from giving up or to give someone else a boost.

As that first afternoon wore on the tropical temperature heated to a point rivaling Death Valley. We were deteriorating fast, not so much because of hunger although malnutrition had set in a month or so before, but canteens were empty and dehydration was beginning to cut men down.

The only cold thing there was the cold fact that Jap guards were murdering our friends in cold blood. When someone staggered and fell, the nearest Jap bayoneted him and seemed to take pleasure in it.

I knew I was in the greatest crisis of my life and that I had to use all of the reasoning power I had and the training I had received to enable my survival. I was enduring as well as most of the prisoners about me except the bullet wound in my buttock kept needling me. I saw that the Jap guards were picking more on the outside of the lines so I decided to stay as near the center as possible. I determined never to make myself obvious any more than necessary.

Prisoners were searched as often as the Japs pleased, especially after the changing of the guards. Our little necessities in our tote bags shrank some each time they shook us down. If they didn't find a Parker pen, a high quality watch or a gold ring we got our ass kicked or our toes stomped.

One officer, I believe a major, was carrying a prized pistol that had been awarded him. That was against all orders, carrying any firearms. A Jap found it. That officer died a terrible death and caused others to die. It was just behind us

The "Death March" begins.

and we kept on moving. We just heard guns firing back there and never knew all that happened. Word like that passed up and down the line.

About that time, possibly an hour later, an older officer broke down and began crying aloud and offering a hundred dollars, U.S., for a drink of water. No takers. I doubt if a drop of water was for sale. Likely a few people had a few drops they'd been thirsting for but saving for a worse crisis. Sorry to say, the old fellow in despair ran amuck and a bayonet finished him.

I am trying to portray the incidents that happened in my sight and hearing on that fifty yards of road that was my little world, moving toward no known end. I have no idea how many marchers were up ahead of me. Miles and miles were behind me I think.

This might have been the third day and men were shuffling and half staggering along. As I noticed the roadside I saw more and more black bloated bodies strewn along. I had plenty of time to wonder who they were, where the empty spots were in homes across America? Why this had to be?

Afternoons were the hardest. We were growing more miserable every hour. I felt my steps getting harder to take and could see it in the prisoners around me. My mouth was dry, my throat swollen and caked. Breathing was getting quite difficult. Faces that I could see were sunburned and blistered just as mine; lips swollen and cracked. Somewhere back there where a Jap had emptied someone's pack I picked up a tube of Listerine Tooth Paste. I started using a little at a time with my finger back on the top of my tongue and in my throat. It helped some. I passed the word.

By now we had lost all account of time. That wasn't important any more. Men weren't talking, just trudging along trying to stay alive. A few days ago one could hear a prayer occasionally, hear the Almighty's name called. Not anymore. At present we walked part of the time in a sort of daze, similar to sleep, hoping if there were guardian angels they might give us a little ease from this hell. I guess it helped. Something kept us walking.

A man screamed a few yards up ahead, just out of my sight. We were getting acquainted with misery in every feeling and sound. That was someone getting a bayonet. We knew what it sounded like when a gun butt broke a man's neck, knew how a Jap set his foot in a man's chest and kicked him off his bayonet, then wiped the blood off his bayonet on the dead man's clothes. We were learning savagery by the hour. Those slant eyed bastards were always right along-side of the column, yelling, yapping like hyenas and always ready to put another notch on their bayonet. This was victory? Time seemed to drag by so slowly.

Eyes that weren't seeing much stared ahead out of grimy, dust caked faces. Mouths were partially open and at times gasping for breath. We walked in a road strewn with human feces and blood. The stench was terrible. Each of us 24,000 American captives were unaware that we tramped a unique trail of history, only that now we were walking alone on that

The march continued—for many, it was endless.

crowded road fighting a personal battle for capacity to take another breath, for the will to take another step. Each shared his pain, confusion, thoughts, his fears with none; nor could he.

It was as if we were on automatic pilot and some latent instinct or unknown source of energy furnished enough zeal to take the next step and another, gave us reason to know that if we had any future it was on up that road somewhere and that we wouldn't make it without an Olympic effort. Survival urges kept pushing listless legs. Surges of anger and hate might have played some part in motivating a few weaker moments. But I wouldn't discount some prayers from back home that might have touched us.

I don't know their reasoning but the Japs let us bed down on the road one night. I felt somewhat rested but not invigorated. Several rifles fired as we tried to get up on our feet the next morning. I guess some fellows back down the road were too sick to try anymore. Getting back to traveling with all of our stiff, sore muscles and joints was just too much of a task. Making it through the next few minutes took our total determination. It was that kind of journey. We were all fighting for our lives and death stayed just one step behind us. One short lapse and one joined the men lying beside the road.

It might have been at the end of five days on the road, maybe six, I wasn't keeping count, when the section of prisoners I was in started moving off the road and was directed toward a large wire enclosure. We were served what a little, goofy, squint-eyed Jap interpreter called a meal. It consisted of a ball of rice the size of a baseball. Nothing else. Then we were told to bed down.

A line of men began forming where a small stream of water trickled out of a rusty pipe. I spent more than half of my sleeping time sweating that water line. When I finally reached the water I drank 'til I vomited. Then I drank some more, filled my canteen and found an empty spot where I got a few hours of sleep. Some men were upchucking their rice balls they had gobbled down. Others were eating it. Under drastic enough circumstances a man will do anything to survive. After all, on this road only the fittest survive.

We hoped for more of these stops but it didn't happen. After about a week we were semiconscious and barely keeping on the road. Groups of a half dozen or more began joining hands for support. Just the touch and grip of a fellow prisoner was therapeutic.

As time went by more men were failing and falling to their death. They got the bayonet. Hardly an hour passed that some barbaric behavior didn't occur within my sight or hearing.

If someone wishes to measure suffering by counting casualties, here would be a place to begin. On the Bataan Death March one could count approximately one hundred per mile on an average. To count another way, near one thousand a day of America's fine boys and young men were left dead alongside that road. But to know the soul anguish in any one prisoner, a person would need to walk in that prisoner's shoes the same number of hellish miles. One's estimate of heroism and bravery can change with one look at what the Japs left along the highway out of Bataan.

One more picture before we reach trail's end. Somewhere back along the march Filipino women and children would gather and toss small pieces of food or offer encouragement to us. Japs were evidently jealous and would fly into a rage, beating, shooting and bayoneting some of them as they fled. Natives dared not be American sympathizers. At one such place a little boy about five years old stood with a big smile on his face and his little fingers spread with a "V for victory Joe", showing a child's compassionate heart. A large Jap soldier ran and kicked the little fellow right in his middle. We knew he was dead when he hit the ground. I don't think I saw a half dozen Japs that displayed any conscience at all.

After eight maybe ten days I heard coarse rasping voices up ahead trying to say, "We're here. We've made it." And so we had made it to San Fernando, P.I. But that was only the first stop on a long journey through three-and-a-half years of Jap prison.

That was nearly sixty years ago and I fail to recall many things of importance readers might like to know that happened on the Bataan Death March. I'm sorry. Also, will you pardon an eighty-year-old man if he chooses to keep a few secrets forever?

17

A Train Ride

I remember something about arriving at San Fernando but not much. Short, scattered memories that were related to the horrors of the road keep coming up like snapshots. I was in a daze, without reasoning ability.

I'll share some of these flashes the way they come to me now.

Water. My mouth, nose and throat swollen, parched, cracked and open sores...There was water...Water!

On my knees... My face almost on the ground, strangling... Pure hell....

Rice... Two men carrying a huge basket... The sight of rice balls nauseated me. Had to eat just a few grains at a time... Made myself....

I wanted to urinate, bad...I couldn't....

Aware of hot sun. Had to find shade....

I still can see the men coming in. Staggering, holding to each other...more dead than alive. I don't know where they all went...Something just steals sight and sound away....

Legs awful sore and stiff. Charlie horses....

I was afraid...afraid to lay down...afraid to sleep...I awoke. I guess I went to sleep anyway.

Oh, how painful to get up— I thought my bullet wound was getting infected ...I hoped I killed that son of a bitch...anger and fear just came and went.

Time went by...over and over the same old thing...every day.

Probably a week or more went by. I don't remember but I had some time to rest and mend and become more aware of the multitude of men that had made it.

My pants were blood-caked at my right hip and some man asked me about it. He washed the place and rubbed salve on it, then dressed it. What a gracious soul! I wish I knew who he was.

Acres of men lay over the area, at least getting rest, a ball of rice now and then and water. Precious water. Complaints of every kind abounded. Sore, blistered feet, aching used up bodies but everyone suffered most from dehydration.

In much too short a period a long string of boxcars came rattling in. Jap guards were kicking men trying to get them up when getting up was the hardest thing to do. Some men would never get up. It was their journey's end, perhaps hundreds of them.

Then a battle of wills began, to be or not to be. A few of the worst cases decided they'd rather die than move. Those rifle-packing bastards made sure they didn't do it at their own leisure. They prodded the boxcars full. When every man that could be packed in standing up, was in, they slid the door shut. What a hideous torture chamber experience.

It seemed hours before the train moved out. Men were already vomiting and being vomited on. A new experience of not having enough air would be killing men ere long. After we were moving, some oxygen came in the cracks but not near enough for that many people. I had been shoved without mercy into a corner where I could scarcely move a muscle but a small, bursted plank let in enough air for me to survive on. I hadn't had many breaks on this trip but oh! Precious Guardian angel.

All in all, this was the most vicious part of our prisoner experience to date, a half day of terror on wheels. It was becoming more evident that the Japs didn't intend for us to live.

There was no reason to believe that those men in other boxcars were making it any better than we were. Finally wheels started screeching and cars bumping each other. At last we were coming to a halt. Then doors rolled open. This is a scene hard to put in words. Men were in such cramped condition they were incapable of body control. Most of us just tumbled out on the ground. Many were passed out from lack of oxygen and some were dead. People who have not suffered such hardships can't imagine the price that today's freedom cost.

It took all of us using every ounce of strength and ability we had left, to get men on their feet and moving. We had very little mobility. Japs were going wild with laughter at our inability to function. We were getting angrier and more frustrated. My opinion is the anger saved us, gave us a reckless ambition, a little extra drive for the moment.

Of course when the fun was over the Japs began their usual threats and screams and prods attempting to get us into something similar to marching formation. We were doubtless on another march. Two, five, ten miles, who remembers or cares? No one felt capable of it but the memories of the six or eight thousand men left on the roadside reminded us that it was those who pushed on beyond their strength or ability who were still alive.

Getting started taking steps again was like life and death fighting for the final say. The bayonets left scars on many of us. Some measure of time before reaching O'Donald Prison Camp, a nice platform had been built beside the way where some Jap "Big-Wig" officers stood. We were motioned to circle around so we might hear every word said to us.

After several attempts to quiet us down and get our undivided attention, a little, bow-legged General came quick stepping out of a limousine parked nearby. His staff stood stiff as timber and screamed for us to pay homage by bowing several times as they did. Little General had enough brass on his bosom to sink a boat and ribbons of every mixture of colors like he was fresh from Japan.

The man stood up before us and yelled things in many different keys, loud and squeaky. His interpreter squeaked a little finer than his boss, passing on his threats to us. We were told we were all going to die and that they would help us liberally. How much Japan hated America was told over and over. He said that, "We Imperial Nipponese have some incredible surprises planned for when we invade America." He said Japan was more than capable of conquering the world and

Little General bragged of other conquests such as Korea, China and the Philippines.

After a good hour of bologna pushing he concluded and his staff took turns brow beating us with some oriental crap like how much greater Japan was than America and how we couldn't fight. Little General departed in a limo that was smoking profusely. It seemed doubtful to me if either of them would survive the present war.

Hours later, more dead than alive, this group hobbled into O'Donnell Prison. More than half of them would die there. We had grown not to expect much and we were not disappointed. O'Donnell was a hell of a place for American Service Men to have to slowly die in.

18

Prison

The dictionary says prison is a place of confinement for criminals. We were an army of soldiers that our country officials had used, starved and dumped on an island without any way of escape. The Japanese captured us and didn't want us. They couldn't make us fit into their plans so they committed us to O'Donnell Prison. That isn't the whole story but will suffice for now.

O'Donnell was a deserted American Army camp with a new barbed wire fence around it. The buildings were built of bamboo and covered with grass. Barracks were built in the lower level ground and officers quarters above on a slightly higher area with plenty of room for officers' staff and attendants which was understood to be off limits for the underlings.

I don't know what went on up there. There were American doctors; some at least. They didn't even come down to see the privates die. Perhaps there was one. There were about thirty chaplains, both Protestant and Catholic that had every opportunity to identify with the suffering masses and at least say a prayer over the dying ones. They didn't show. I didn't see them there, not once, with words of encouragement from the Bible or any other source for that matter. Where were you fellows? Perhaps God won't ask you that. Maybe He will.

Come to think of it, we didn't have funerals for any of those fellows up there, the elite, at least not in our burying trenches. I wonder what they had to eat that we didn't or medicine to take

The condition of inmates of the camps deteriorated quickly.

that wasn't available in the low ground? A few words now and then from our officers might have helped. There weren't any wire fences between us. This is my opinion only.

Barracks were close together with a ten-foot lane between each row. Straddle trenches were dug out at the end of the rows which was a long way for many men with dysentery to have to run many times a day and night. Who could expect a very sick weakened man to run a hundred-yard dash when he had an urge to go? Consequently the path to the straddle trench was strewn with human waste a hundred or so times every night.

Men died at those straddle trenches and in them. They died all along the filthy trail. Eventually ten or so feet around the trenches were as filthy as the inside. Barbed wire was covered an inch thick with flies. Dysentery was a killer that was thinning out our population.

Malaria claimed a lot of lives. Men were so run down with little immunity to disease that they were dying fast. Mosquitoes were everywhere giving us injections of malaria. Some fellow said he heard two mosquitoes talking the night before. One asked if they should eat him here or take him across the fence and eat him. The other replied in the negative. If they took him over there those big ones would get him. Having no quinine made malaria hard to deal with among such mosquitoes.

Rice was cooked in a caldron seventy-five or so yards above us once each day. Oh, how good it smelled. Each man had a number instead of a name. That was Jap policy. Each number got a scoop of rice and his number recorded. Unfortunately men were loosing their appetites and would lend their number to other fellows. Some didn't have the will to walk, or crawl the chow line. I found out pretty quick I could get another helping with someone else's number.

Even though Bataan and the death march was behind us, a person could never fully heal, especially under prison conditions. We had lost weight so gradually and hardships had sapped our strength until we were emaciated almost beyond recognition. Extreme stress on prisoners' minds and wills since we became victims of so many Jap atrocities was too much to overcome. But most Americans just don't die easy. I did everything I could think of to heal and gain back strength.

Not a leaf or blade of grass was visible in the whole compound or within human reach under and beyond the fence. Quan cans (canteen cups) were all around cooking little taddicks of grass, weeds or even grass roots. We tried. Oh God! How we tried. To an American just half a chance is a fighting chance. Men were dying everyday by degrees with so many enemies to face.

Malnutrition and beriberi became hard factors to deal with. Two kinds of beriberi plagued us. There was a dry kind that was most painful as it ate the nerves out of our feet and legs. And the other kind, more and more faces became swollen beyond recognition. Feet and legs were so swollen that some bursted and water dripped out. So many obstacles to overcome, they outweigh a strong will to live.

There were a few rascals in camp who stole, cheated and overpowered less fortunate victims, without any conscience, they meant to live at any cost. These crooks were soon black listed and brought down. There are many means of delivering justice even in prison.

Rumors constantly toured the barracks. What we didn't know for sure we were always surmising. One thing we knew for sure. There were two classes of people in this prison. One class was living well and apart from the poor class. The majority was poor and getting poorer. Suspicious minds were liable to snoop just to make sure of what might be going on amongst the elite. One big piece of evidence was up at the gate. Filipinos were selling black market food, which should have been ours on Bataan. Canned food, cigarettes, they were all American Stateside stuff. Who had money to buy such luxuries?

I wonder what happened to our company funds? If all of the outfits whose governing body lived up there in those quarters together had their company funds, they were set up for a long duration. All outfits had operating expense money and I was told some had payrolls that the men didn't receive after war broke out. This money had to be somewhere.

I heard two theories on how they got money through the Jap searchers. Some carried money in their shoes or in bags fastened in their crotches. Others said stashes of it were buried on Bataan and it was later brought by Fhilipino confidants. I have no idea how they got it there but some got through.

The burial detail—every morning the dead would be gathered up and carried to a ditch about 150 yards below the camp and buried.

19

The Burying Ditch

It wasn't a decent burial but it was the best we could do for those who were passing away each day. A dozen or more were able-bodied enough and respectful enough to dig the ditch each morning, then gather up dead bodies over the camp area.

Most of the dead were clad in dog tags which identified them. Meskits or some other item to eat from was their only possession when we found them. Clothes were scarce items and whoever the thief was that stole clothes stole personal items as well when a person died. There was not enough of anything to go around. If a prisoner had any plans for the future, he had to be a scrounger but not a thief.

A Jap guard took the burial detail about a hundred and fifty yards below camp and pointed out where a ditch should be dug. We dug it seven feet wide, three feet deep and as long as it needed to be to accommodate that day's burying.

We returned to camp and began gathering up the dead from over camp. We had stretchers or litters innovated from panels or siding taken from nipa barracks then unused. Four men, carried the litters on their shoulders. These prison camp hearses were the only ones involved in a burial service. Even though there were twenty or more Chaplains in camp they evidently didn't give a thought whether prisoners had a decent Christian burial or not. I didn't see one at a single funeral. I grieve about that to this day. I hope some Chaplain began that service after I left O'Donnell. I don't know.

One of the most heart-rending sights I have ever seen was as we passed down the outside of the wire fence toward the burying ditch. A cluster of prisoners gathered on their side of the fence. Some held others up, some held on to the fence. Those who could were saluting. Those who could were weeping, but everyone paying homage in his own way to fallen comrades.

I've wondered what that sight looked like from Heaven and what the reaction was there? Words weren't enough to express the grief and heartache that cried out for deliverance inside that prison wire.

By the time the burial detail reached the burying ditch they had previously dug; it was already filled with water because of the proximity to sea level. The dead were dumped in and held down with poles while they were being covered with dirt. We always placed their dog tags in their mouths. The best we could do wasn't good enough sometimes. Shallow graves full of water made it impossible to cover every one well. Rainy weather washed some out and animals fed on them. We couldn't help that.

We honored the hopes that America would come again some day and claim Her own, and would deliver as many as possible of these dear soldiers to the right gold star families back home. American prisoners were just beginning their sentence under the Japanese and we thought a lot about home. Mom's cooking filled our dreams but it didn't do much for hungry stomachs. Day dreaming was the greatest pastime we had, reliving the good old day's back home. Sometimes I breathed a prayer for my family, wondering if I could make it back there sometime when this war was over.

That desire was possibly the strongest force motivating me and others to dedicate ourselves to service. It was a constant battle

20

Once Upon a Mountain

The most ambitious men who fought for survival the hardest, stayed stronger than others. Every survival technique I used or saw back in Appalachia became a practical blessing. The use of plain old country horse sense got me past many bad places. Keeping my mouth shut and watching what was really going on, even acting ignorant, gave me some advantages.

The Japs took men out of camp from time to time on labor projects. From those who returned I found they had to work hard but the percentage of deaths out there weren't as great as those who stayed in camp.

What seemed to be an important detail was being picked from the best prospects available. I cleaned up, straightened up, I borrowed a small comb, wet my hair and beard. It wasn't easy to get the kinks out but I at least looked better, and tried my living best to look able. I was chosen along with thirty or so others. This was another step in the dark but I just had a feeling to go with it.

We left O'Donnell by truck and were taken on a back road to Bagio. Bagio had been the place where American brass had gone on extended vacations and everything they wanted or needed was there for the having.

Prisoners were given orders to clean the place up. All of the bottles were practically empty at the bar. I found a can of something that had lost its cover. When I sneaked out back and beat the top in with a stone, it was asparagus. I ate the whole thing. I haven't eaten asparagus since.

Bagio was a vacation for us. We had three or four days of rest and enough rice. Three of us found some flour as we were cleaning the kitchen and I made us a pan of gravy for our rice.

One memory that comes to mind was what must have been Lingayen Gulf. As we passed there a huge black battle ship was anchored a half mile out in the China Sea. Wow! It looked like the middle of the world; like the dividing wall between me and home. To hell with it, I thought. Some American will pull the trigger on you one day.

The trucks we rode were different from any we'd seen before, not too different from other GI trucks except its fuel. Two metal barrels about fifteen or twenty gallon size were attached to the front of the bed. Pipes, tubes and other attachments made them look like some functional part of the truck. A pile of burning wood (small sticks) was at one side of the barrel that had a door somewhat like a heater. After inquiring around some, a Jap explained to us that in one barrel the wood was smoldered into charcoal then more wood was added. The smoke was filtered through the other container and then into the motor producing horsepower. It didn't create much but enough to do right well going downhill and fair in level ground but on an uphill grade we had to jump out and push right often. The best one could say about the contraption was that it traveled on less energy than a wagon which could get by with one or two horsepower.

A Jap truck was loaded with packs, bags and bundles of their equipment. Each prisoner was made responsible for one package weighing from thirty to fifty pounds. We each shouldered our load and left on foot on an ox cart road going north. This was another one of those sweat and blood deals it was beginning to look like.

A huge mountain range rose up in front of us that would defy well men to challenge. Towering peaks and long high mesas looked arduous indeed. Native trails began branching off and leading toward the lowest gaps between mountains but always gaining altitude.

The mountains in the Philippines are formidable. The trails are steep, winding and chocked with vegetation–in other words, a jungle.

The higher we climbed the more dense the jungles became with tall spreading trees and typical Tarzan vines. One type of vine bore a fruit looking object that smelled heavenly to hungry men but the sweet smell had deceived us and it was hollow like a gourd.

Loads of rice and other food for the Japs as well as metal objects known only to them made tiresome burdens, obviously enough for an extended journey. Two meals of rice a day wasn't an adequate amount but was more than we had been used to.

Not more than four days had elapsed when we were taken by surprise, or better said, bushwhacked. Previously we had heard that a group of Americans and Filipino Scouts had escaped with all the supplies they could muster on their backs and vengeance in their hearts. Guerillas were the last things we expected. They caught the Japs off guard too but they put up a good fight in a well-chosen spot where the Japs didn't have much cover but the guerillas had a little rise in their front for protection.

57th Infantry (Philippine Scouts) Fort William McKinley; Rizal, Philippines. October 8, 1937. This panoramic photo from the National Archives show the unit on parade.

Several Japs were killed and wounded in that one-sided battle but we had been walking behind the Japs and quickly used our packs in front of our prone bodies. Most of our wounds were superficial. Firing soon died down and the guerillas disappeared. Four Japs stayed with the dead and wounded while the remainder went guerilla hunting. They weren't gone long.

They buried their dead and patched up their wounded but did nothing for wounded prisoners. We spent two or three hours there, ate and moved on. After nightfall they pretended to bed down but left us there and moved as silently as possible back into a thick wooded area. Just in case guerillas returned, we were their shield.

Next day we divided up into three groups of twenty, more or less; twelve or fourteen Japs and eight or ten prisoners going up three different trails. Prisoners had no idea what the mission was but the Japs had discussed something that seemed to be very important for an hour before bowing and grunting the usual rounds before parting. Just from a privates' observance, their courage level was somewhat low. It seemed that they divided somewhat grudgingly.

Details at this point begin to be faded and hard to remember but I believe that the senior Jap officer in each squad was riding

This unit "surrender" at the cessation of hostilities, however, many of the men became "guerrillas" that harassed the Japanese throughout the occupation of the Philippines.

a horse. I know that there were a few horses involved. A little Jap plane began circling us several times a day. Japs were strung out up the trail with us prisoners behind. The elevation made climbing harder and harder for us.

Our path took us through small barrios or villages sometimes twice a day. Inhabitants were always gone; news evidently traveled a fast grapevine up here. Anytime we reached a village near evening, the Japs spent the night there. They had the luxury of the shacks while the prisoners stayed on the ground beneath them. Shacks stood six to eight feet off the ground and from evidence, chickens and pigs ran free everywhere. Japs pissed down through the cracks in the floor making it unsafe underneath. A decent place to lie was out of the question but just the shelter was welcome. We pack animals were always tired and uncomfortable, having to choose the best of two bads.

One morning we had just picked out a gap between two mountains and started toward it. Our narrow trail dipped and circled into a deep ravine, which was bald except for weeds and head high clumps of bushes scattered about. Straight across the ravine was a steep bluff facing us covered in the same vegetation.

When we were halfway down the ravine we could hear a wild stream below us. A few yards farther down and the steep bluff facing us looked less than two hundred yards away. Yes, we got bushwhacked again. Small arms fire broke out over there and bullets were suddenly spraying all around us. We couldn't run. We couldn't hide. We couldn't even surrender. Japs commenced firing over that way although they couldn't see any targets. Those guerillas had us dead to rights. None of us prisoners had ever been this tight between a rock and a hard place before. We were desperately trying to hide among our enemies and were being besieged by our friends. Both Japs and Americans got stung a few times but nothing serious.

That little telltale plane was up there circling and had directed men from one of the other groups in behind the guerillas and they began firing. Up went the white flags and a man called across to an officer on our side asking for surrender privileges which was granted.

The guerillas came down in a group directly toward the river out of our sight. Some officers broke out a bottle of sake and started celebrating their evident victory. Fifteen or twenty minutes elapsed but no prisoners appeared. Jap scouts were sent to investigate. No luck. The guerillas had vanished into the abyss downstream where a Jap dared do nothing more than look.

We pack animals celebrated silently with poker faces and took the wrath of Imperial Japan with something close to dignity. One fellow said the Japs didn't dare hurt many of us or they'd have to carry their own damned packs. Yelling, kicking and stomping our toes made life more miserable for us.

21

A Near Human Surprise

Not many pleasant experiences became a part of the ignoble prison lifestyle. We can remember the hard painful days, deprivation, anxiety and hunger. Trudging the aimless roads we wondered if we would ever be rested, well-fed and pain free again.

Thoughts of home and pleasures that were timeless helped time seemingly go by a little faster. We tried to shrug away from memories of prison camp horrors and the conditions there but the memories kept returning. Our friends and comrades there were praying for food every thinking minute of the day. Perhaps we can't live by bread alone but we'd trade anything for it.

Scaling these mountains day by day was awesome and to us it was labor without meaning. One afternoon we hiked into a small village that was empty of people as usual. A little field of corn looked just right for roasting-ears. An old mother hog and a gang of three-month-old pigs straggled around through the village giving us prisoners hunger pangs. What a potential feast was there for the taking.

The Japs weren't hard to persuade. They began sniping at pigs that wouldn't stand still, laughing and teasing at each other's poor marksmanship. Everybody got involved, throwing stones, slashing with sticks and diving at fast legs. Occasionally we'd hear a pig squeal that had made a mistake. That old sow got angry and protective, making chomp-chomp, growling noises. She ran an officer up some steps into a cabin. What fun! Everyone laughing. War and hatred was forgotten momentarily. A Jap soldier killed the mama hog. Loud laughing, a child-like concerted effort trying to collect supper that was squealing, running, dodging, well-educated in not getting caught ensued.

Using every method we could think of, we finally had the animals all in a pile and we had accomplished something together. We were humans for a while, a unique occasion for us all.

In a few hours we sat down to a banquet of pork, rice and boiled corn ears. I gorged myself just like everyone did on the best, most welcome meal I can remember. Oh, what a joy!

Next morning started the same old manner of life that was so typical of those double-hearted, schizophrenic bastards. There were other mountains to climb and perilous occurrences up ahead that we would have to endure but had no way to prepare for. I think we just hardened ourselves to face it and tried not to cross the bridge until we got there.

22

My Best Friend

James Helfrich was the finest Christian young man I was privileged to know in prison. His witness and counsel brought hope to many waning souls. We got acquainted aboard ship on our way overseas.

A few days after the pig feast we were loaded and tramping toward another tall mountain range. As the group crossed a creek, James lost his footing on a slick stone and fell, damaging an old hernia. James was in terrible pain. Two of us prisoners took our turns under his arms bearing him along.

Shortly after reaching the next village a Japanese service man that was in our group introduced himself to James as a sergeant someone and explained:

"I am a good surgeon. I will give you the best surgery possible to make you well again." James agreed. He had no other option.

Surgery took place in an old nipa hut. Very primitive would explain all aspects of the surgery, very primitive.

Anesthesia, yes, five men held James until he passed out. He stayed unconscious throughout the entire procedure. Under such circumstances one couldn't expect it but it was a miraculous success story.

The Japs had some plans to work out or decisions to make. We never knew what, but after three days we were on the trail again. James recovered rapidly and was soon keeping up without any struggle.

These are typical of the type of houses found in the uplands of the Philippines.
Of course when we saw them, they were deserted.

23

Prayer Time

Drizzling rain at such a high altitude made traveling very awkward and uncomfortable. There was enough mud to make slick places, enough rain to soak us soggy wet. About an hour before dark we came into a village with fifteen or twenty bamboo houses. They stood eight feet above ground on bamboo legs. Villagers always left before our group arrived. These empty shacks were especially welcome shelters in such disagreeable weather.

Japanese chose to occupy the best and give us the ground underneath as always. Even though my blanket was wet I wrapped it tightly around me. I had the cold shakes for awhile but heated up nicely before long. I was sitting against a post reading a small bible I carried when I looked up and saw a large Jap standing over me. I expected trouble but not so. Signs and body motions were language sufficient to get our thoughts across. My bible was evidence that I was a Christian. He had been involved in some Christian training somewhere. He got it across to me that his future life as a soldier didn't look good. He expected to be killed and asked me to pray for him. One of the strangest sights an observer could ever have seen was a Jap soldier and one of his prisoners of war on their knees together in prayer, the Japs' rifle laying between them.

When the soldier arose, we gripped hands and he departed. On his forehead there were two-dime size scars about three inches apart. I had seen Jap soldiers with this type of scar up and down their backs but this was the first one I had observed on a forehead. It was evidently some superstitious practice mothers had of scarifying their children. I believe it was burned.

Rain eased during the night and the sun came out bright next morning. It was a very cool, brisk morning and it was so good to be alive. Conifers shared a clean fresh odor. Small flowers sparkled on the ground. How gloriously blue the sky was as if one could see an eternity beyond the horizon. Those squalling, nagging voices of our captors always brought that same, old feeling of half-anger, half-hate right back, polluting the beauty of creation with negative spirits. But for now it was their little world. I knew some mountains they would never climb back in the Smokies, not while I was alive.

Native Filipinos—the Japs may have invaded the country, but the jungles were still in the hands of the natives.

24

The Forks of the Road

Following the plainest trail, which led around a large bald butte, we came upon another very open area where visibility was good for a mile. Just in front of us was a fork in the trail. One prong led off slightly downhill to our right. Twenty yards in that direction stood a tall pole and on its top was a human skull. Its meaning spoke loud and clear, both American and Nipponese.

Those Japs didn't even have to think it over. Their leader pointed in the other direction. No one objected. We hadn't eaten that day so in a hour or two we stopped to cook rice which they rationed out to us prisoners rather liberally. After filling ourselves we prisoners chatted about the day's exciting experiences until I guess it was three or four o'clock in the afternoon.

From where we were we could see at least a mile toward a large mountaintop. Little flicks of light caught our attention there and in minutes a line of them was stringing out down the mountainside toward us like a string of diamonds trickling along rather fast. As the front of the line came nearer we saw human beings scantily clad with dark wooden shields and spears honed so bright the sun played tricks on them. When these head-hunting savages became so numerous we couldn't count them, and them coming right toward us fast, I guess we all figured this was it. I'd been scared in this war of nerves, but nothing like this, and I didn't even have a stone to throw. We couldn't even demonstrate, much less communicate. The show was all theirs in their territory and we were frightened spectators.

One Jap officer gave an order and we started marching straight toward them. Their line swung under us about a hundred yards and they completely ignored us, seemingly intent on something ahead. We were relieved for the moment but we were fed up with this crazy stuff; had our pants scared off enough till we were sure we could never learn to cope with it. Being scared to death one is just as dead as being speared several times. Believe me, I have seen Japs who were smelling scared too.

Our trail turned down toward a deep hollow which we followed for perhaps a mile before we intersected a freshly traveled trail. It was easily obvious that those native warriors had crossed back under and had come this way. The Japs slowed down considerably and were deliberating what to do when we came to a high bluff overlooking a huge meadow. Below us there were gathered, what looked to be a thousand of those strange people.

This trail we traveled would lead us down around the base of the bluff, then directly into the meadow. Whoa! Not that. Seeing that multitude down there was no guarantee that this confrontation was over. Shrubs and dwarf bushes gave us coverage where we were compelled to wait the night without food or sympathy. We weren't close to being friends during this crisis even though we sat close together.

A heavenly sunset kindled a great mural aflame over the mountain horizon but beauty didn't calm our mortal concerns. We watched action beginning to take place below us that was transported right out of prehistory.

At late dusk a bonfire was started out in the center of the meadow. Fuel had been gathered for the last hour or two and had been deposited in a huge pile. The bonfire was kept ablaze that night being fed from the deposit.

Some person started a slow chant, just hacking away in cadence. Slowly others joined in. Then circles, three or four of them one at a time born, one clockwise and another

They danced till the fires burned out. One of the many war-like people native to the Philippines.

counterclockwise. Within the hour that mass of savagery was caught up in intense fever of religious passion. They chanted and danced. Chanted and danced in an episode of mania that no civilized human eye had seen or ears heard. I know this is unbelievable just as other incidents I record are, but not one man present that night will ever forget how we got a glimpse of pre-history right before our very eyes.

It might have been a tribal celebration, a yearly or possibly once in a lifetime ritual and revelry. All I know is that that night was the most dramatic portrayal on record of what science says we once were.

It continued till the fire burned out and in the morning's early hours they slipped away fatigued, leaving the meadow empty and quiet. I can imagine there will always be ancient spirits hovering over that meadow, but thank God the participants had gone their way and we were still alive and untouched by cannibals.

Our presence in their territory did not seem to be a threat. But the Japs and Americans who lived through a panic attack on that memorable night have all had more than one of those midnight movies we call "flashbacks."

That little spy plane with the rising sun on its side made its usual trip over us next day. The Japs had broken out an antique radio device. Parts from several of our packs were assembled. Prisoners took turns cranking a generator that evidently powered a radio. They took turns squawking and hollering to the pilot, no doubt relating their horrible experiences. We prisoners laughed under our breath about how comical those people could be in their present condition. I wonder what Tojo might have done?

The "decoration" on some of the housess in the deserted villages would make a man shiver.

25

Jungle Horrors

The further and higher we climbed into a great mountain range the fewer small villages occurred. Dense jungles and deep ravines hid the most primitive people we had ever seen or heard tell of. Narrow trails almost always graded toward lower gaps.

The last empty village we came upon was a revelation. As in houses we had passed, clay-cooking hearths were in one corner of the one-roomed houses. Soot made black the walls all the way up to an outlet in the roof. We were used to seeing pods of pepper and other dried objects strung across the corner above the cooking hearths. All were as black as the wall.

Here, four or five houses had jawbones strung across, human jaw bones. From two up to eight in different shacks just hanging there, black as sin. I got cold chills running up my spine, crawly feelings that were virgin to me. I had no desire to become a human trophy. Stories of missionaries being boiled in a caldron had been somewhat of a joke. Now it seemed highly probable. I felt a little too welcome here. Japs were posting guards and walking around with their guns at ready; acting real human. They knew what wisdom teeth looked like. We spent the night there only because it was almost nightfall. I hoped they trembled at night.

Before sunup we were hiking toward a group of bald topped mountains and plateaus. About noon we topped out on a long bald plateau. A few little scrubby bunches of bushes grew there but mostly weeds from waist to shoulder high covered both sides of the trail. Patches of tall, wide grass that natives used for clothes and covering their houses grew about.

The group had hiked to approximately the center of the bald area. Suddenly without warning a hundred or more natives were standing all among us. Japanese and Americans were buddies in a heartbeat. Caught with their pants down the Japs dared not raise a gun. Savages had us dead to right, enough strength to wipe us out and none of us spoke a word of head-hunter.

Those natives had been camouflaged in their grass hats and capes, squatting all about in the weeds around us and suddenly stood up in unison. What a surprise!

We removed our hats and bowed to them, as courteously as we knew how and grinned, we couldn't smile. They removed their broad hats and capes, clad only in "G" strings and seemed to accept us as friendly. Whatever their purpose was, they certainly got their point across.

Their men were a bit smaller than we were and muscular but none obese. Females were tattooed around their fingers, arms and bodies, even their breasts. They looked almost as if they wore knitted sweaters that reached down to their "G" string. Sun and weather had left their bodies wrinkled deep and thick in appearance.

We bade them goodbye. Japs and Americans walked closed ranks and never looked back. I wondered if this was the last we'd see of them? I wondered if this was the time of year they might be particularly hungry? I was grateful to the powers that be that we were moving once again.

There was nothing we could see that might be edible up there in that barren wilderness, no visible means of livelihood, no reason to exist there. I think we all felt like we had invaded pre-history.

26

"At Any Cost"

A fter about two weeks of climbing over mountain trails up and around three, four and five thousand feet, we seemed to be on a slow descent and circling toward the outside of the main mountain range. Prisoners were getting more footsore and weary. Japs were getting sore tailed and grouchy, worse all the time. They had killed two of our men yesterday for reasons unknown and threw them over a cliff.

We were seeing some of the ill tempers they portrayed on the "Death March." Only a few days ago they were sweating blood when natives accosted us, but now they were kings of the road again. We couldn't understand their mood swings. They never let us forget for long that we were enemies.

As we slept one night in a dense forest and had been bedded down three or more hours, I awoke with an awareness that something strange was going on.

I thought I heard a slight noise behind me. When I raised on my elbow and looked back, a man had crawled up to within two feet of me, head to head. He instantly whispered, "Fear not, I am a Filipino Scout. I am with the guerillas." How in the name of goodness did he know I was an American? A week ago they were shooting at us.

I was apprehensive and disturbed. The Filipino continued, "My commanding officer wishes to know what the Japs' mission is up here on this journey." I could think of nothing more than that they were writing notes and drawing sketches of some kind. I asked for the privilege to escape and join the guerillas but the Scout silently vanished into the dark shadows.

Two days passed. Every minute was wringing me out. Feelings I couldn't identify nagged at me. I was eager to escape. I tried to act normally, knowing in my heart that the Filipino would return. He did that night. Just like the first time he came, but this time I was waiting for him. His message was brief and like a bomb exploding.

"My colonel commander orders you to destroy the literature *at any cost.*" That put me on death row in a heartbeat. I had some serious questions to ask that bird but he was gone in a hurry. I felt like yelling. I called him names, the ugliest ones I knew. It didn't stop my trembling. For hours I felt like puking. This just wasn't so. It couldn't happen to me. I wasn't the one. Someone else maybe but not me. There were bigger, stronger ones.

Jap soldiers were yelling insults of some kind when I awoke and I didn't feel like being insulted. My mind was asking questions that I couldn't answer. Why didn't that son of a bitch do the job himself? What right did that band of renegades have to get me in trouble? Who did that colonel think he was to pass a death sentence? I rebelled. Then I caught myself wondering how I was going to do it. Every once in a while I'd try to yellow out and couldn't.

After hiking till about noon, reason eventually quieted me down some. I'd been hot under the collar. I thought, my percentage of making it till the Japs were whipped, was in low figures; possibly not at all. Would I, should I trade that slender possibility for the chance to save numbers of American soldiers sometime when our home team came fighting back? Then I figured, a job can't be called big or little or expensive if it was really necessary and a soldier's honor was challenged.

I found myself expending energy, precious energy, trying to stay up as close to the Jap column as I dared. I had my eyes on an easygoing young officer who was wearing the bag that I was to destroy "*at any cost.*" Over the long run I was convinced now that the price was right. Inside I began to quiet down, even to anticipate the moment. The will to do overcomes the odds, and the danger, and fear. It does not eliminate them, just dominates them.

Nothing counted any more except an opportunity where I wouldn't bungle the job. I would know when. Weak as I was, the only question I asked, am I able? Then doubt; short lived.

The Japs were following a trail down a steep hillside toward a river that was white water as far as one could see. It must have been thirty yards wide. A trail was visible up the far side. The senior officer on his horse tied a rope to his saddle and gave the drag end to Jap men who held hands with the person behind them, forming a line through the fast water. Prisoners were behind the Japs, staggering and stumbling in the treacherous current. Water was straddle to belt deep, sometimes more.

A young Jap officer was left to bring up the rear. As I took his hand I was trembling like a leaf because he was carrying the leather bag. I had made it a point to be on the rear of the line of prisoners, next to him. No one expected problems but me. As we stepped into the water I was trying to pray. I tell you now, its next to impossible to pray when you're about to kill someone.

Our end of the line had reached halfway across when someone lost footing and several swung around and down. It created a sort of crack the whip situation for the officer and me. We were loose in the deepest, fastest current. I thought fast and came up for air, still ahold of his coat collar. At that time I stripped the leather shoulder strap from him and came up for air again. I had my left foot on his back. Up to this point I had no idea what was going to happen. I had no definite plan. He was ceasing to struggle and I was thinking fast.

I saw an old tree trunk with a few short limbs sticking out in the water down about forty yards away. I knew I had to get to that tree with this Jap. He was the only ransom I had for my life. Two minutes, possibly two and a half, we were back on land. That current had been treacherous.

When the Japs reached us I had the lieutenant out on the bank belly down and was giving him some old-fashioned lung pumps. He was coughing and gagging but coming around pretty fast. I fell over completely exhausted. That current had gobbled us up and the Japs were chattering like monkeys trying to figure out what had really gone on. I could pray now.

Back on the trail those demons were debating what to do about me. I didn't have a name, I was a number and I could hear them saying my number often. The lieutenant passed by me and whispered, "arigotto," his word for thank you. I nodded my head.

After about an hour of marching the senior officer climbed down off of his horse and motioned the other Japs around. He spoke his piece and climbed back on the horse. He had passed sentence. I could read their actions too well. I was sentenced to die.

Both Japs and Americans were traveling up the trail. A little Jap private we called "yard bird" had grabbed hold of me and turned me around facing back down the trail. I heard two other Japs talking for a short space of time. One evidently spoke to "yard bird" just as he hit me with his gun across my upper shoulders. I thought he had killed me. I was staggering in pain. My eyes were in and out of focus. I almost passed out. The ones I had heard talking had sent the "yard bird" on up the hill.

One of the Jap men laid his rifle stock against me and slapped it hard, loud enough for those on up the trail to hear and know he had finished me off. I fell in agony; I opened my eyes just as he looked back. He had two white spots on his forehead.

I couldn't see the other man very well because my vision was blurred but well enough to know he was taking a pistol out of a round holster on his belt. He walked over and pointed the pistol down at my body. I closed eyes ready to say "howdy God" when he fired. Twice more he shot along my side. I blinked my eyes and looked him straight in the face. He was the lieutenant that I pulled out of the river. I whispered "arigotto." He nodded his head and I was left there alone, I thought to die.

I wasn't sure I could make it. Partial consciousness was coming and going. I was getting worse. I don't think I could move. No, I wouldn't live like this. "*At any cost,*" he had said. It wasn't cheap. I don't think I regretted it, even as painful as it was. Duty and honor I think are brothers. I brought something with me from my mountains like that. I still had a little of it left, just possibly enough to see me through this emergency.

27

Buzzards

Nightmares kept changing scenes and dimensions. Pain throbbed in my head. My shoulders felt paralyzed. I panicked, so afraid, deserted and alone. Every time I was conscious enough to see, there were those big black birds sitting in a nearby tree, not like they had come there to roost. Silent they were except two or three of them kept flying down occasionally to determine if their next feast was dead enough to eat. Their wings made flapping, swishing sounds close enough till I could smell their stinking breath.

During a few minutes when I was aware, I determined to live. Surely those bastard carrion eaters wouldn't start on a man before he died? There were lots of things a man would rather have happen to him than a covey of those skinheads cleaning his bones. I tried to yell but I don't think I did. I tried to wave my arms but I guess I couldn't. Then night again. I dreamed Mom was praying for me. She was saying words I couldn't think of. More nightmares. More vultures investigating. Pain kept trying to steal my life away. If a dying man ever fought for his life, I gave it my best battle.

Hope touched me with tender hands, rubbing my aching back and shoulders. Oh, guardian angel, looking like a head-hunter.

Strange words spoke to my fears. One of the two pieces of cloth the stranger wore was a headband. He went somewhere

A head-humter

nearby to where water was and wet his headband. The water that cooled my mouth and throat was oh, so welcome and I didn't worry once even how dirty or germ infested that piece of strange cloth was. I'll never doubt guardian angels again. He must have left then.

I stayed a little longer after that. Over and over the nightmares returned. Night kept crowding me, smothering me, robbing me of myself. I struggled to live. Every conscious moment was a prayer. Possibly each instinctive movement or struggle was contending for Divine aid. Some answers we may never know.

But I knew when he returned. I was burning with fever. Trembling. Weak. A rebellious appetite tried to refuse the herb offerings he so kindly pushed down my mouth with his fingers. It must have been his kind of medicine.

Water dribbling into my crusted throat brought me around for a brief time. Horror filled experiences came and went minute after weary minute sapping my strength away. Then some restful moments gave me the first peace I'd had. Shortly I slept without aggression. More herbs continued to come when my benefactor visited. The native also brought some kind of food.

Days slipped by. Small objects under me dug into my hips. I was tired. Slowly I recovered with the constant aid of a savage looking human and his knowledge of mountain medicine. His food was evidently nutritious but not what I felt like I'd want as a steady diet. Compassion from the least expected source had strange healing qualities that I will never cease to be grateful for.

Many pieces of evidence we had seen along the trails we traveled would cause one to believe this person and hundreds like him who lived here in these mountains were head-hunters and at times ate human flesh.

From whence came the kindness that gave me my life back? I have no way of knowing the source of that beneficent force but I'm certainly glad the native wasn't hungry.

A week, two weeks or three? One day the last group of Japs and POW's came into sight. I had hoped for this and tried to condition myself toward that end. Else, I had hoped to make contact with the guerillas. I was ready for the same old grind with the Japs again. I told them I had been very sick but was now waiting for them.

My guerilla friends had not bothered to find out if the order had been carried out or what the "cost" had been. I reckon no one will ever know the whole truth but me.

This story was not an isolated incident. Scattered over Jap dominated country, many, many Americans made similar gifts to America, each in his own strange way. Some, possibly most, didn't live to write about it.

Days later we reached a little town where Jap troops were stationed. We were given the same food and similar quarters as these Japs. What a surprising way to recuperate five days. Then we were put aboard trucks and journeyed back to prison camp. They called it Camp Three, Cabanatuan.

Surrender of U.S. Troops on Corregidor. The men on Corregidor did not have to make a "Death march," so they arrived at Cabanatuan Camp Three in much better shape than the rest of us.

28

Leaving the Tropics

Back in the prison camp, I had only a few items to call my own. A canteen and canteen cup that I would have died defending, a small Bible and a tin of quinine were my total possessions. The quinine, I lifted from a refrigerator as we passed through Bagio. I could not read the Jap writing on the tin but a Jap officer inspected it when it was discovered later on and returned it to me without comment. The Bible I took from a table where two others lay in a house where a missionary lived or had lived. That little village had definite outside influence on its appearance. No one was there. My eating utensils I would not loan to anyone but my bible and quinine I liberally shared.

Camp Three, Cabanatuan was much better than O'Donnell had been when I was there. There was very little future for the commoners at O'Donnell. I'm glad I had a fighting chance on the mountain detail. Prisoners have told me that one other camp Cabanatuan was not much better than O'Donnell was.

Number Three had fewer deaths per day but some were still dying daily. Some prisoners walked about barefooted, their feet and legs swollen from beriberi almost to the point of bursting. Faces and hands were bloated until their own mothers couldn't have recognized them. One could see men walking aimlessly with no expression on their face, emaciated yellowish pale. A few just sat and stared. For them, the war was over. Percentage wise there were more that could be termed able-bodied here than any place I'd been up to now.

Then, there were two social levels, two lifestyles, distinct ones more here than at O'Donnell. The Filipinos had come inside the fence and set up a small commissary selling State Side food and cigarettes. Rumors were making their way around without any hindrance that sex and gin could be had. I don't know. Rumor and suspicion aren't evidence. But I did see a man I was quite sure I knew who had grown a beard to hide his double chin. Some prisoners told there were two or more hundred men living high on the hog up there on "king hill." I don't know.

I'd still like to know what happened to our Company fund and how much of it, if any, had found it's way into the black market and who had paid for those Camel cigarettes Jap guards were smoking? Some of the business going on here made me think of a story I read about a poor hungry fellow sitting at a rich man's gate and didn't even get his table scraps. Yes, he starved to death there and someone went to hell for it.

Men can't live on a bowl of rice a day and can't heal without medicine. I was having a hard time making a comeback from the Jap gun-butt between my shoulders. But I hung around up near the upper crust. If there was anything loose that might be had by slick hands, it would be up there. Someone set a small out-house aflame one day and fleeced a poker game when the players left to fight the fire. That helped a lot.

An Indian prisoner from California named Glenn Jim lay across from me in a barrack. He was having a terrible fever attack. Malaria is a killer. I remembered my quinine pills so I started him on a course. He objected to begin with but I assured him he didn't need money. It broke up his malaria attack. Jim was working somewhere for the Japs, doing washing, cleaning and other labor. One night I heard something rattle like a canteen cup handle on the shelf over my head. Jim was just coming in from work and had brought me a cup of stew with lots of meat in it. That was the best stew I ever ate. Another best was a bond between two prisoners meeting each other's needs.

I had about two good weeks with enough food and rest. If anyone caught on to how I was getting food, I never knew.

Jap officers began making rounds through camp jotting down prisoners numbers, asking questions, checking the health of the best looking prospects for some work detail. The first week of October 1942 a large work force was named. I was one of the fourteen hundred chosen.

I am reminded that on the eighth of that month we climbed aboard trucks and were transported to pier 7 (I think) in Manila. Philippine women were trying hard to feed us. Caldrons of goat meat cooked in the background. We each got a small helping sometime that night with a helping of rice. Many details are vague as I look back. I could be wrong on some of these details. I'm sure I have been on others.

The *Tottori Maru* was docked there and next morning we boarded her. She was a Jap freighter, which showed sign of long usage. The horrors we prisoners suffered aboard that ship earned her the name of "The Hell Ship."

Jap soldiers goaded us down into the hold with bayonets and gun barrels until we had only sitting room so close no one could move. There were no facilities for our needs, which we couldn't have reached if there had been.

Before we got underway, heat was causing breathing problems. Before the day was over we were starving for water and were sitting in our own body waste.

Once a day we got rice let down into the hold in five-gallon metal cans; enough for a small ration for everyone if it got around. Time after time it got shortstopped by piggish Americans who tried to get their ration and stash some away.

The same problem arose with the water. Two or three men were helping each other cheat. All three got hit in the head one night with a heavy object. Inequities had to be taken care of in the quietest way possible. A court of necessity seldom had to pass judgement but occasionally when the general welfare of prisoners was concerned sentences were passed, individually.

I believe there were three holds occupied by prisoners. It was found out later in the journey that a large area in the ship was filled with Jap soldiers being transported back home. That accounted for us prisoners being packed in such cramped conditions.

An honor system was about the only law we had. When a man died his personal effects were understood to go to the most needy. Under such horrible conditions, things got out of hand and two or three men ended up with valuables that belonged to everybody who had any. We knew who the thieves were. Those rascals were up falling all over people at night, pretending to be out of their mind, crying and apologizing, but we caught on. One man told a "traveler," that's what they were called, "I'll know you the next time I see you" and he slashed his face with a small piece of mirror he had. That incident and a few more similar ones got the rogues under control.

We were survivors and respected each other enough to do what was necessary when need arose, especially for those unable to cope. Generally that was true. Any time someone went crazy yelling mad, Jap guards would shoot randomly into the hold, sometimes killing innocent men and wounding others. Being scared half to death didn't help much either. That was another sad chore we were forced to take care of. How any of us lived, I have no idea.

29

The *Tottori Maru*

Y ou want to hear about prison, just listen for a few
minutes. We were touching someone on every side and
couldn't move in any direction except stand up. No room.
My short pants were stiff and sticking to me all around my bottom
with dried dung. I sat in puddles of other men's urine and mine. I
wasn't sure what that was on my hands and places on my face.
Other men were no better off than I was. There aren't enough
descriptive words in our language to tell how we felt.

There aren't enough devils in hell to know what we thought.
We were so dry and dehydrated, so on the verge of insanity at
times that there wasn't any hope for things to get better.

You know what 90° heat is? It was 95° outside or more we
believed. I don't know how hot it was inside with all those
people in there and no ventilation, possibly 100!

Some people started screaming on topside, "Torpedoes!"
"Torpedoes!"

That was the best end I could think of at the moment. No
one panicked in our hold. A little Irishman started an Irish
song in a beautiful tenor. Some started remembering well-
known hymns and we hummed and tried to sing along. A
strange mood came upon us. A spirit? Maybe. For a few
minutes our miseries were less bad.

Tottori Maru had a narrow escape we heard. As she turned, a
torpedo passed on each side, very, very close. Even the Japs
didn't know we had submarines in the China Sea at that time.

Top: The S.S. Pampanito, *one of the submarines that the Japanese did not know were operating in the China Sea.*

Right: The survivors of the Rakuyo Maru *are rescued and taken aboard* Pampanito. *The* Rakuyo Maru *was transporting British, and Australian POW from Indonesia to workcamps in Japan when it was torpedoed.*

Photo by Paul Pappas

The incident gave the Japs some conscience. Large white Jap writing was painted on the smokestacks. We were informed the message was "Prisoners Aboard." The *Tottori Maru* and a number of other ships had taken refuge in Formosa. Big brass came aboard and was yelling orders. Small sections were let come up on topside and we were washed down with water hoses till everyone got doused. We were fed better. Rice and pieces of fat pork a half inch square were dished out to us in our soup. Man, did our appetites ever come alive. But lots of our men were too sick to eat. I saw some of them dumped in the China Sea.

They didn't clean the holds and we were crowded right back down into the same old shit. We must have spent four nights there while the Jap Navy was out swabbing the China Sea for allied submarines. One consolation, we could breathe better.

Reading what we heard and felt, *Tottori Maru* was underway. The atmosphere was changed a little. They left the hatch over us completely open and the temperature was a little cooler. We had some ventilation. No one knew our destination but we hoped it was near.

I'm telling this story the way I saw and felt and remember. I'm sure others would tell it differently. Some even kept diaries and their rendition should be more accurate. The biggest question I have with the whole account is how people, Americans, could endure almost unto death and then recover over and over and over again. I wonder if we have that kind of fortitude today and what would happen under similar adversity?

Just after dark we were made aware we had gone nowhere but were entering Tykow Harbor in Formosa again. Jap thinking. This time we stayed several days before venturing out again. I'm not sure the Jap Navy was doing so good out there sub-hunting. Even at this early point in the war they exhibited something more than caution, namely cowardice. One little submarine had them all stymied.

In harbor, the Japs were a little more thoughtful and possibly somewhat more liberal due to those high-ranking officers who would appear with no notice at all and yell. The crew came alive like jumping through a hoop. The officer gone, they passed it down to us. We caught hell on the rebound.

At sea again after another week the misery started coming in a different way. Prisoners began chilling at night. We were leaving the tropics and had no clothes suitable. Our living quarters were more like a floating privy on the high sea. God's name was used hundreds of times a day but not in ways to make the place sound religious. A few did pray. Others cursed, mumbled obscenities about America deserting them. Some moaned because of pain but seldom did one hear an intelligent statement or sentence. It was cold and getting colder.

I try to pick out incidents of a positive nature when there are some, but on *Tottori Maru* all positives were low positives or positively negative. If the reader could feel the conditions for only one minute, smell what we lived in only a moment, then realize we were prisoners under these animals three and a half years, you'd realize I'm suffering through that experience as I write this, very similar to horrors we knew them. One difference, I'm not hungry or thirsty or suffering much bodily pain. But it puts my soul in turmoil.

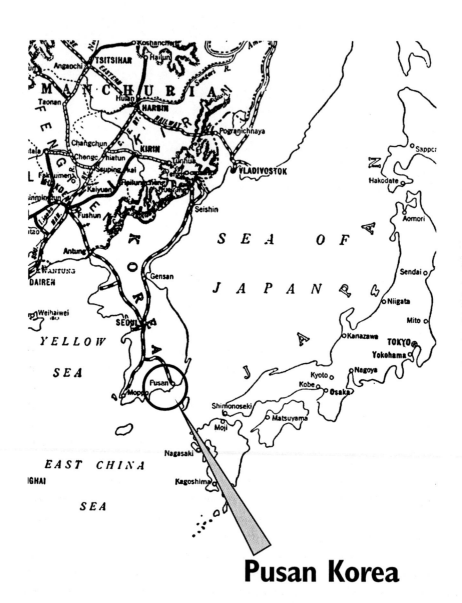

Pusan Korea

30

Pusan Korea

Pusan Korea was single digit Fahrenheit weather. We were frigid. Two hours after we docked there, we staggered, crawled, fell and drug someone out if we were able. Above all of our miseries, we intended to bring everyone off of that floating out-house and down the gangplank.

Every prisoner was aground again but shivering like an onset of Dengi Fever had struck. None who weren't there could imagine in a lifetime how painfully terrifying this hour was. We were three side by side in a line. The middleman was being almost carried with his arms about the two outside men. All the way down the line, even outside men were stumbling along but sharing what little energy they could generate.

The line was directed to a shed where a large furnace like affair was and every stitch of our clothes went into that furnace. We left there in our birthday suits, fresh born naked in terrible November weather.

Korean old women were passing out clumps of soap. Some nozzles were spewing water and we had a bath, shivering scrubbing, stumbling, but excited of all things. No one seemed ashamed. Even the Korean old women didn't seem excited and possibly looked in pity. We scrubbed until we were as red as the flaming rectum on the Jap flag.

Next, we struggled along through a small hall into a fumigation chamber. It burned our eyes and noses. Someone said later it was something like DDT. Not many more minutes and we'd be clean, disinfected, Hollywood nude and ice cold dead. The whole group was trying to keep moving, their teeth chattering and bodies shaking like a leaf in a storm. Fourteen hundred men can't do anything in less than an hour but at this stage, time was of the essence. We were simply frozen blue and had to do something fast.

A miracle of great consequence opened up, a door into a warm room. The head of our line, which was double file, was directed down each side of a long table piled high with clothes. First was two piece underwear, long handled. No time to change, just move, move, move. Suits of clothes came next, winter clothes like the Japs were wearing. Shoes were second hand but had been repaired. I snatched the largest pair I could see.

What looked like a huge assembly hall gave us place and time to dress, exchange sizes and jabber like on Christmas morning. As soon as we got thawed out and dressed for the weather, we started a new time of healing. Absolutely nothing of these dimensions had happened to this group of prisoners as gratifying as getting clean and clothed, not even half.

Fellows doubted, figuring that these Japs were too deceitful for us to be confident. There'd be a catch of some kind. They were baiting us for some reason. They'd hook us before this was over we all believed. Japs were very un-trustworthy and that is an understatement.

For another surprise they sat us down and fed us, fed us rice, large salt pickles, ugly piles of seaweed a foot square and other things we couldn't stomach. We feasted but not much. Our stomachs wouldn't accommodate a full meal. Dog-gone-it!!!!! Those salt pickles set our mouths and throats afire anyway.

Some sort of business ceremony went on for an hour or two. We were turned over to some other branch of service. Two well-dressed business-looking men seemed to take us over for some unknown reason. At least these surprises had given us a better frame of mind but we were still in bad need of rest and healing.

Almost a month I think, had elapsed since we left Camp Three, a nightmare we'd like to just erase out of our lives. We hoped and doubted and wished those new people might give us time, food and whatever else it would take for our bodies to recover and our nerves to settle some. We'd give someone their money's worth if only they would treat us half-way decent. A small meager hope we were dreaming, not like a great comet but more like a firefly blasting off with his tail burner glowing.

The Japs had shifted gear now and were showing some purpose for a regiment of many times beaten but never whipped prisoners.

Words like "manchuko" and "hoten" were picked from Jap conversations that we listened to. It didn't mean much till a train rolled in and we were made to board it. A trip up the entire length of Korea didn't enter our minds. Our train had wooden bench seats made of slats, both bottom and backs, square and flat both ways. Some things were just made less comfortable than others and we knew every degree of discomfort in a personal way. Radiator style heat gave a new meaning to comfort. Up to then we were riding high.

Two rations of rice a day wasn't enough to brag about but it kept our stomachs from growling. I started to take a nap but I felt something too familiar. Just as sure as shootin' trouble was back. Body lice had invaded our new clothes and my comfort level went down like the evening sun. I started examining myself and I had those little cannibals crawling all over me. We were familiar with them. Tottori Maru was polluted with enough of the critters to stock a blood bank. The very thought of sharing my future with those crawling bloodsuckers was intolerable. The only gratifying thing to me was that the Japs had them too.

A rumor whispered it's way around that we were in the process of becoming factory workers. I had serious doubts that many of us could recuperate enough to do much of any kind of work. Having been drained of weight, strength, ambition and courage, our bodies would take more time and food to obtain a normal working condition.

Japanese bigwigs began some propaganda about pay and better food for those who produced in their factories. On the other hand they explained that there was little future for those who didn't. What a word of encouragement! Mukden, Manchuria was just ahead.

I can't remember leaving the train and hiking to the old Chinese Army Installation where we would live. All of the barracks were buried half underground and were covered with a foot of dirt and sod. Walls were double and insulated with sawdust. Dirt floors. Wooden bays elevated a foot high on each side of the dirt walkways reached from one end of the room to the other. Straw tick mattresses lay close together on the bays.

Once again we prisoners faced wintry cold weather but this time constantly sub-zero temperature. I am aware that I have written so much about suffering and deprivation that readers will be skeptical, but I haven't over-told the misery dished out by the Japs. If anything, I have saved the reader many instances of personal atrocities too heinous to describe. Even the almost sudden change from the tropics to Mukden, Manchuria, where the temperature went from $0°$ degrees Fahrenheit to $45°$ below in two weeks, would be quite a shock to anyone. More than four hundred prisoners died that first winter and I'll give you details of that ordeal later.

Production had dwindled at the Jap war factories and their war effort wasn't getting good reports from Tokyo. The factory owners and operators of MKK a five factory complex, were in trouble. Someone got a bright idea to use prison labor. That is why we were in Mukden, Manchuria. In my opinion the Japs had cut off their nose to spite their own face by killing Chinese workers and working them to death. Little wonder they ran out of productive work hands. We saw many of them sitting along the road dying by degrees. No work, no food, no home. It was many, many times worse than I am telling it. Thousands and thousands of their best Chinese people had been worked to death.

Americans were put to work producing war materials of many kinds such as airplane parts and supplies. After the first winter only about a thousand prisoners out of the original fourteen hundred, were alive and able to work.

31

Zero Ward

Being in rundown condition plus two or more old wounds that made a round trip ten mile hike each day and work at MKK Factories an impossibility, I turned up in a makeshift hospital.

One of the old barracks had been designated by the Japs as a hospital. It had no doctor, no nurse, no medicine, no care of any kind. Its main purpose was not a place to be rehabilitated but a place to die. This establishment was divided into three sections. First was a long room where a majority of the patients resided. Most of us gradually grew worse. One American Doctor who had no medicine, came by and would sit with the dying ones and would attempt to encourage us all.

The center section was the latrine and on the other end was Zero Ward. Zero Ward was the last chance end of the hospital. The worst terminal cases were shifted to that exit point. Just outside the "door of no return" was an antique warehouse kind of place, which they used for a morgue.

During winter months bodies were stored in the warehouse which was called "Ward 13" and stacked up like cordwood, naked as they came into the world. Doors were not fastened out there and at times patients could hear the wind crashing the doors back and forth.

Two more able prisoners whose job it was to transfer bodies from Zero Ward to Ward 13 told of how they found a body in a crawling position just outside the morgue. He was naked and frozen ice stiff after crawling outside. Those two men swore they didn't know who put a live man in there. Other horror stories too terrible for home folks to know were stored up in a prisoner's memory.

James Arrington and I had lain side by side at the end of death row in Zero Ward. So far as I know, we were the first men to walk out of there alive. We weighed less than a hundred pounds each. Two mountain boys we were, grew up less than twenty miles apart in Western North Carolina.

After the war was over we each returned home, married and had families. But we were not free. We spent years in the hospital a month or more, sometimes six months at a time. Post traumatic stress and anxiety problems had kept us from being what we might have been. Prison life was always a part of us, constantly plaguing us with nightmares and flashbacks.

A few years ago I stood over James in his church to eulogize this very dear friend. As I stood there in the pulpit looking down at his flag draped coffin, Zero Ward suddenly flashed back so real I could still smell my own rotting body just as it was then, feel the same desperation and even hear the doors slam on Ward 13. Time had turned backward and for a few moments we were there again somewhere between life and death, fighting to survive. Now for the first time he was free. He had found rest.

I wish I could portray a few hundred American service men who were making a real fight to survive before Zero Ward but for most all it was a futile effort. Bodies waning away and spirits devoid of hope, growing weaker each day, was a sight to make angels weep. We all knew what it was like to feel death coming on. The following is the fight I put up prior to my going to Zero Ward.

One evening two men from the galley came through our ward with a small wooden bucket of boiled carrots. I hadn't seen a carrot in a year. The men were passing them out to some patients. My whole life was a sudden prayer for one of those carrots, just as if one carrot would save my life. They slowed down in front of me and one of them said, "Aw Hell, don't give that son of a bitch one. He'll be dead before morning anyway."

My mountain anger blew and it did more for me than a bucket of carrots. I swore vengeance on those men and on the whole prison system. I started eating everything that resembled food that I could beg, borrow or steal, a bite here, one there, a dead man's last meager meal he had left, I took. Any unattached bite of food I took.

Barely able to creep about a few steps at a time, I had one aim; find food and get it. I had become a cold-hearted survivor determined to win this one or die trying. I started too late. I fell in the floor and was dragged to Zero Ward, the most dreaded place in existence outside of hell.

This was not the whole story by any means. A ghastly plot to annihilate the weakened sick ones was one of the Japs most cruel blows. This story is fully authenticated by the 104th Congress. It is the hardest story I've tried to tell so far but I'll give it a try.

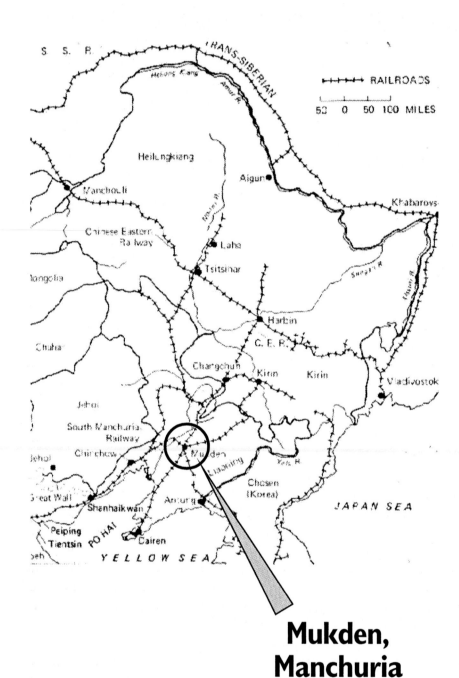

**Mukden,
Manchuria**

32

Dr. Ishii's Clinic

Dr. Ishii's Clinic was a Jap experiment station located a few miles north of Mukden. It is now a well-known fact that he and his fellow scientists conducted barbaric acts, which they called, experiments on Chinese people, white Russians and prisoners including Americans. One of their projects started in our hospital barrack.

Up to three hundred men were given what we were told was vitamin shots. They were not vitamins. Those shots were loaded. An outbreak of amoebic dysentery almost immediately started bowel cramps and diarrhea. Most of that group died during that winter. A Jap guard making his round one-day explained, "no work, no profit. No profit, you have to die."

So they had infested us with an Asian strain of amoebic dysentery and we were called "logs of wood" in their records. The main room of our "hospital" was filled with very sick men. Prisoners who deteriorated fastest were transferred to Zero Ward. Our latrine, which served both large rooms, contained six five-gallon metal cans. That was all. No paper, no cobs, nothing. Those cans were supposed to serve several hundred men who were visiting there every fifteen to thirty minutes, many of whom made it only part way there.

Before any night was over those cans were full and overflowing all over the dirt floor. Body waste covered our feet to our ankles. There was no way to wipe, no where to wash. Thousands of body lice were drawing blood samples from all of us constantly. Malnutrition was coming on fast. Beriberi, two kinds, was destroying some of the finest young men America produced. Boils, sores, pellagra, scurvy, all of this and bowel cramps that didn't produce anything but mucus and four or five inches of anal–prolapse. A silly "yardbird" walked through every day or two with one vitamin shot to give someone. I remembered a sleight of hand trick which looked as if I removed a finger at the joint. Needless to say, I used that magic for vitamin shots every time. He was easily amazed. Right often one or two of Dr. Ishii's henchmen came by to inspect their experiment. I wonder if they observed Ward 13? That was the bottom line.

Those slant-eyed bastards were draining every drop of humanity and life out of hundreds of Americans who couldn't lift a finger to prevent it. I got word that my good friend, James Helfrich, was dying and I used all of my strength and will power going to his side to say so long. I don't know how I made it. He was talking to his folks gathered around the table in Ohio. He was eating his mom's cherry pie with homefolks. Soon he left the pain behind and went to his long home. I returned to my pile of straw and tried to cry but I couldn't. I didn't know how any more.

Chinese men came each morning and cleaned up the privy. They were "honey dippers" who were middle class farmers using human wastes for fertilizer.

I have already told how I fell in the floor and ended up in Zero Ward. A scuttle butt got around that a Jap doctor and an American had teamed up and were beginning to use simple treatments, old Chinese remedies, and common sense practices but they didn't have any medicine. They even came to Zero Ward. Just a visit from them was like a vision of heavenly beings. After a brief consultation with James and I on the last two pallets, the Jap doctor said, "You need charcoar, rots of charcoar." He saw that we got charcoal. Lots of charcoal. I remember sleeping. I'd been sort of afraid to sleep, thinking I might die in my sleep. I wanted to be fully aware. That was one thing the Japs couldn't deprive me of. I awoke to a bowl of soup (100% fat free) and a small piece of bread. The old saying that a dying man would grasp for a straw was about right with us.

Dr. Shiro Ishii

Three weeks, four, five, quite a while calendar time and pounds of charcoal later the two of us, James Arrington and I, leaning on each other walked slowly out of Zero Ward. Outside, the charge of fresh air was therapy that could only be described as a new birth out of the womb of despair.

The following is about Dr. Shiro Ishii and unit 731.

The July, 1996 issue of our XPOW magazine, "The Quan" contained a 104th Congress House Resolution dated May 1996. The following is a quote from that document:

Whereas in Mukden Manchuria the Japanese bio-chemical warfare detachment unit 731, commanded by Dr. Shiro Ishii, conducted experiments on living prisoners of war which included infecting prisoners which they called "logs of wood" with deadly toxins including plague, anthrax, typhoid, cholera and a dozen other pathogens.

Whereas of the 1,500 United States Prisoners believed to have been held at Mukden, at least 260 died during the first winter of imprisonment and of the 300 living survivors of Mukden, many claim physical ailments related to being subjected to chemical–biological experiments.

Whereas after World War II, Dr. Ishii and other prominent scientists and physicians of Unit 731 who conducted human biological warfare experiments, dissected living prisoners and froze prisoners to death for purposes of scientific experimentation, were given pardons by the United States Military Tribunals in exchange for use of their experiment records.

Whereas these experiment records remain classified by certain Federal Departments and agencies of the United States and access to such records has been denied to the Department of Veteran Affairs as well as to doctors of the individuals who were subjected to the experimentation.

So the good old United States had their hands in the murder of prisoners of war all the way up to their elbows. I for one have suffered through the years from those beastly experiments. Access to those ill-gotten records might have saved hundreds of lives and untold amount of suffering.

The Commission also signed away all of the Prisoners of War's rights to claim any reparation for forced labor or brutal treatment at the hands of the Japanese. I did without those things but when I see "Old Glory" waving I know it was just another bit of payment I made on the freedom she represents and the pride I have for the people of America.

Asheville Citizen A2–Wednesday, May 21, 1997:

WWII Germ Warfare Victims found in China

Beijing–Buried in big, earthen pots, the remains of Chinese who died in Japanese germ warfare experiments during WWII have been found in southern China, state run media reported Tuesday.

Reports of the graves came as a group of Japanese rightists, many of whom claim such atrocities were never committed, arrived in Beijing for meetings with Chinese scholars, officials and students.

In 1994, a Chinese historian reported he had uncovered evidence that as many as 20,000 WWII refugees died from germ warfare experiments conducted at Zhongshan University.

Chinese and Hong Kong War refugees, long thought to have died of starvation and illness, were killed by various infectious diseases planted by the Japanese researchers, the 1994 report said.

(This is also proof of Japan's savagery.)

33

Making a Comeback

I found some sort of stick I could lean on for support as I walked to my old barracks about sixty yards away from Zero Ward. Sergeant Graves saw me coming and came out to meet me. He was the barrack leader and was ready to help anyone who needed him. As we went into his end of the barrack it smelled heavenly. Meat was cooking.

We ate lunch together, the first dog meat I ever ate. It was a good first step toward recovery. Sergeant Graves said he had snares set at several likely places around camp. He said the Chinese neighbors had been complaining about their dogs being missing. They ate them too. We saw them patching the fence to save their breeding stock. I was assigned a little activity in and around the barrack, enough to keep me busy as I recuperated. All men, who were able-bodied at all, worked at the factories five miles away.

After a couple of months, good things were beginning to happen. I was growing stronger. I had gained weight up to or above a hundred pounds and going. The winter was beginning to moderate some. Temperatures were staying above zero. The Sergeant caught us another dog. Meals were rationed out in his barracks by him after it was carried there from the cooking place. The wooden buckets had soup for the evening meal. It was nothing like Campbell Soup. It was mostly water made tasty by winter onion tops, a few carrots and a few beans. Sometimes the soup was thickened a little with some sort of grain.

Sergeant Graves said if each man out there got twenty beans, he wouldn't ever know that he had been shorted one bean. That would mean forty beans extra for him and me. I was crazy about his arithmetic and I thrived on it. He was always talking to the Jap officers about giving us more food. The Sergeant had a heart as good as gold. He was an old Army man with an above normal head on his shoulders. I wonder what happened to him?

As spring came on, my health was improving and my instincts were prompting me, "It's gardening time." An urge kept me aware of the outside and of similar times back home. Our survival back there depended on a large garden, well balanced by years of experience. That was back home. This was Mukden Manchuria, half way around the world from home. But I ventured out there. I found a place I felt like was a garden spot. Oh, I knew I would never have food growing there but please don't take a prisoner's dreams away from him.

Dead weeds were shoulder high. I found a piece of wood and slew them, not all at once but a few at a time. I was exhausted when I had an eight-foot by eight-foot clearing. Little hives of gnats were beginning to swarm around. A small white animal came out of a pile of logs at the end of a rotting building and stood up, looking around with spring in his countenance. Birds ventured out sounding like it was time again to mate. Yes, there was spring awareness in all living creatures.

More than a half-mile away the railroad caught my attention when I heard the unmistakable sound of a train engine approaching. Dreams of another sort bore new desires in my bosom, desires of freedom and home.

Then an engineer that was a professional got ahold of the whistle cord, blew that train whistle every way that a train whistle could be blown. It literally tore me all to pieces. I fell on my face. Pent up emotions enough for any one person's life time boiled over in my soul. I was making noises I had never heard before, uttering words that made no sense, feeling pangs of anxiety born of extreme prison anguish. A prayer of faith reached somewhere out there like a beam of light and anchored. I could make it now. Oh, how I wanted to go home!

34

Moved Into Town

In midsummer 1943 we prisoners were moved to a new facility within a half-mile of MKK, the factories where prisoners worked. That was four and a half miles closer than before and made other convenient differences. Factory owners had been building those new living quarters for us ever since we arrived in Manchuria. Now they were finished and everyone moved in.

Three brick two story barracks stood side by side equipped with latrines and laundry rooms, such as they were. A nice hospital building stood nearby but was unequipped. We had a galley with three large caldrons already set in a furnace. A shop for camp upkeep, which was poorly supplied, at least had workbenches.

Japanese had housing and office space aplenty, fifty or so yards away from us. They had a dark room over there too, not for photography but we called it a dungeon. It was exactly three steps one way and two the other, inside. It was never summer time in there. Frost covered the walls worse than a refrigerator. I'm sure some sadist gloated over that addition. A prisoner had to keep moving day and night to stay alive. He got a blanket, a ration of food and a canteen of water every third night. The cooks took him hot water. That wrapped with him in his blanket warmed the prisoner up and rested him during the night.

A thirty-foot high brick wall surrounded the compound with a guard tower at each of the four corners. Twenty feet inside the tall wall was built a six-strand barbed wire fence. Jap guards walked between the barriers periodically. One gate controlled all of the traffic, coming and going. Going out they commanded us to count off to see if we were there. Coming in we shed our outer garments and were searched for any "contraband" that might be hidden on us. That meant if we had off brand cigarettes, (black market), small tools we had been working with, or any other questionable articles, we got the dark room. For most any infraction of rules, a prisoner had to serve time there.

Hiding anything from those Japs was impossible. They were past masters at thinking like a crook. But just leave it to an American to find a loophole. If a man had questionable items on his person, he kept it in his hands and stretched his arms out at his side. They couldn't see it if it wasn't hid. Those Imperial Japanese never did catch on.

Working prisoners were fed twice a day. A dipper about the size of a Vienna sausage can was used to ration out our morning corn meal mush. We each got a single unsweetened dip of the yellow stuff. Factory workers got a thirty-minute break at noon but no lunch. At night we had soup. The kind of soup depended on the time of year or if the Japs were disturbed about something. One could safely say that it would be ninety-percent water. Other than water it would be one hundred percent fat free and low calorie. Chinese cabbage with winter onion tops and a few soy beans made up the other ten percent.

Occasionally when things were going their way and they weren't hearing bad war news, soup was strengthened with a mite of thickening, which we presumed, was malo maze. In summer our soup contained sweet potato vines and carrot tops for a change.

Chinese people wouldn't steal. They were honest people. But if we stole some small items that were hot on the Chinese exchange, they would take them and bring us small morsels of food in exchange. Light bulbs, screwdrivers, pliers, nails and any other needed articles were very desirable on the black market.

We each tried to have our own Chinese friend, whom we worked with and dealt with. We never knew what we might get to eat because the Chinese were very, very poor but they always brought something and every bite counted to a starving man.

Occasionally we got an egg, a carrot or some things we couldn't identify. Now and then we got chinby. Chinby was some sort of grain beaten almost flour fine, made into thick dough, rolled almost paper thin and baked in the sun. Six or eight pieces the size of a normal plate stacked on top of each other were rolled up to the size of a man's arm. It didn't have a lot of food value, probably, but it was a belly full.

There was some resentfulness toward a few men who worked in offices or close to Jap officials who stayed strong and healthy, and didn't lose any weight. We didn't know anything but we could see. The hungrier we were, the more envious we were. Does that make sense?

It was bound to happen sometime. It wouldn't have been American if someone hadn't at least tried to escape. Three men tunneled under the wire fence down near the incinerator then crawled under the big brick wall through a water drain tile.

An army man, a sailor and a marine had completely disappeared. Japs spread a net that would have captured anything alive. They were going crazy until Tokyo gave them permission to put a ransom on the escapees' heads.

In sight of camp an acre or more of Chinese cemetery covered a hillside. It had been mined and undermined for centuries just trying to find room for one more body, and another and another. Poor Chinese had been stuffed into any empty space in sight. Dogs that had escaped being eaten, had grabbled dirt and cleaned bones, as well as doing everything else that dogs could do in little cavern hideaways or between body boxes. Cavities had eroded in spots where rainstorms ran down and washed dirt away. No man would think of hiding in a hillside of graves, bodies and ghosts. To the Asian mind, no amount of money could tempt him into that nest of evil spirits.

Our fellows hid in those tombs until some of the pressure let up. Then, they headed north with every intention of reaching Russian Territory. They had no guns but had machetes and knives which they used unsparingly.

Large bounties were offered Chinese people who would dare to stop three dangerous outlaws. I wish I knew the details of that last fight, how many Chinese it took to capture them and how they did it. I wouldn't want to see their road strewn with those who tried and failed to capture our American Heroes. They fought their way over fifty miles through bounty hunters.

When the Japs brought those three heroes back, the whole camp mourned silently. Jap guards paraded them around over camp shackled to each other for about a week. Jap officers took their frustrations and anger out on the whole camp. Their three "outlaw prisoners" grew weaker and weaker. Our food was cut in half and we were restricted to our barracks except when we were taken outside for punishment. Standing at attention in the night for hours was the principal cause of frostbitten feet.

Ishacowa, "The Bull" or "El Toro" he was called, was the most heartless heathen amongst the Jap officers. It was him that took the boys out of camp and put them to death. The Bull was responsible for most of the trouble we suffered. All prisoners had frostbitten feet over and over from standing outside for hours in the cold, twenty or more below zero weather. Noses and eyelids were frostbitten too.

Those officers could slap a man's face open with their saber scabbard and they used it over and over when men began to stagger or fall. My nose was broken flat on my face and an eye badly damaged one night when I was so tired and cold I began to slump forward. They afforded me a piece of tape at the hospital and I found a piece of wood. I straightened my nose bone the best I could and taped the wood against it as a brace. It wasn't a matter of whether or not it hurt, it was a matter of being disfigured for life. Every guard that saw me would begin trying to feel my nose and wiggle it to see if it was really broken. I had a trying time. It is still obvious.

The last I heard of The Bull, he was standing on a scaffold with a rope around his neck and an ex-prisoner had ahold of the trigger. I was offered the privilege of being there to participate as a part of the War Crimes Trials but I declined because of ill health. There were those of us who didn't owe them anything anyway. Most of the American Armed Forces were fully paid up when the Japs got us.

35

Activities in Camp

One day a week was free of work at the factories. A person could do his laundry if the water pipes weren't frozen. In the best of times long lines formed behind the concrete wash basins. Fellows who were sweating the lines told X-rated jokes, teased and growled about some men taking double time doing their laundry. Good-natured pressure was always on the one who had the basin, urging, criticizing and belittling his slow poke ways.

During times when the Japs had more pressure on us, tempers would occasionally flare. Being cold and hungry after working all day or having to stand outside in subzero weather for two or three hours at attention, that left us pretty sore-tailed sometimes. One Yank beat me up pretty well one evening before I got a few good licks in. I don't guess either of us remember why. We could tell when the Japs got whipped somewhere, they would take their frustrations out on us prisoners. They used us to whip on.

Four or five men were customarily left in camp during the day for household cleaning duty and in their spare time they could be persuaded to do someone's laundry for a pack or two of Jap cigarettes. They dare not be caught idle by one of those yardbird guards sneaking around. Guards delighted in making a man do pushups until he passed out.

"Jimmy the Wop" ran the maintenance shop (that's what he called himself). Two or three men, who were crippled up a little

Ishacowa was one of the worst prison guards. He seem to take delight in punishing POWs. Known as "The Bull" or "El Toro," Ishacowa was executed at the end of the war.

too bad for factory work, helped Jimmy repair what was broken and fix what didn't work around camp. Anytime a Jap officer came in to get something done, Jimmy would complain that his men needed some more food. "My crew, they hungry. You expect them to upkeep camp on handful of junk a day?" He was a chatterbox, talked with his mouth, hands and arms; anyway to get his point across. The Jap officer liked the old man and would occasionally have a little extra chow sent over, very seldom but sometimes.

One yardbird didn't like something he thought Jimmy was saying and beat him up pretty bad. A Jap officer saw Jimmy and got the story. No guards came around Jimmy's shop again.

There was a special quarters on second floor, barrack two, where U.S. Officers lived. We watched twice a day as a wooden bucket of chow was carried up to them. Most all-else was a mystery existence. One doctor was out each day giving freely of himself, tending as best he could to sick and dying men. One other officer did considerable craft in Jimmy's shop. He built several musical instruments that brought happiness to everyone. Other than that, they sat on their asses and read or slept or who knows what else. They darned sure didn't lose any weight and they didn't show for special occasions like when we stood at attention for hours out in subzero nights.

Another question hundreds of the prisoners asked was, what about the little wooden bucket of food that went up to the officers quarters twice a day. Was it better than our food, did they get more of it, why were they different than us? Did the Japs know this? Why were they exempt from duties and punishments we suffered through the nose to do? Seven or eight of those officers lived there together and most of them were seldom seen out. They looked in excellent condition compared to most of us. The excesses here though, were never as obvious as they were back at Camp 3, Cabanatuan. Only one doctor was worth his salt. The others were like rabbit dung on poor ground. They weren't hurting anything or helping anything. They were just there not making any racket.

How library books, in English, got to our camp, and how the good Captain got the material for his musical instruments I don't know. The blue prints and hardware didn't originate in our camp. I was working for Jimmy at the time and we saw some nice pieces of well-seasoned fir and birch come in. I began to admire and appreciate the Captain's ability to use well what he had and innovate new ideas into his work.

First a bass fiddle and then a guitar began taking shape a little at a time, piece by piece. Some portions were in a press while others were carved and carefully placed into a sort of mold he had created on his table. He shaped some of the work by pouring boiling water on thinly scraped wood causing it to conform to the shape of his mold.

That Captain was an artist and he did this job on his own initiative. The last beautiful sounding instrument he made was a violin. In a little more than a year we had an orchestra. How they obtained strings and other needed parts was also a mystery. Yeah, there were plenty of mysteries. It was small but was an easy listening band played by local talent that was just a notch above fair to middlin'. But we didn't know the difference and didn't care.

Prison life was a little more livable with a performance on our off days. Music replaced the blues at those times, inspired new dreams, and soothed troubled spirits. And when Bill Hugley sang those Texas songs, a little of America thrilled in our breasts, made us tingle with pride.

Other talents sneaked up out of the audience occasionally and added new dimensions to our orchestra. A Tennessee boy made quite a difference one day when he used a comb and piece of paper. A tall West Virginia clown tore the audience off their seats with a couple of old spoons. He almost buck danced one hillbilly to death.

This was absolutely homemade therapy for prisoners who had no way of knowing how long their sentence was. We needed to clap our hands and yell, needed to be free for just a few minutes, of pressures and excess baggage we carried day in and day out. We needed to feel a little bit of home. God bless America!!

36

Mukden with Each Passing Year

Both at night and on free days there was usually a high stakes poker game going on in the upstairs level of Barrack #1. Poker was about all the Jap money was fit for. We couldn't buy anything with it. Paid watchmen kept guard at each end of the building downstairs and on each end at the top of the stairs. Jap guards made irregular rounds through the barracks and when one came in, the watcher downstairs would yell, "Air raid!" Those gun-toting guards knew something was going on but couldn't catch it. Prisoners looked so innocent, bowing and scraping to them and the Japs never caught on.

After at least two years at Mukden the Japs let enough Red Cross food packages come into camp for each prisoner to have one. One article at a time was parceled out to us several days apart. America sent enough to feed us well during our whole incarceration (we were told) but the Japs feasted on it all but that one measly package each. Army C rations, cigarettes, coffee and a variety of other food items were in that package. One of the most despicable things the Japs did to us was to steal from us the food that our country sent to us and let us starve.

Later on we were allowed to write a card home. They told us what to write but we were allowed to sign the card. That, at least, gave our folks back home hope. Some letters began getting through to us. They had been censored until we could scarcely get any meaningful messages,but it was a little bit of America and home. We cherished them and shared with each other, all except the "Dear John" letters. Some fellows got those.

A media organization came into camp and made cards available to us, which in turn would be read on short wave radio stations and could be picked up stateside. I wrote mine and several others that some prisoners didn't want and gave to me. My parents saved a little record they received from someone in California who had recorded one of the Jap broadcasts. I still have it. Negative messages were not allowed, but I buttered the Japs with good old American flattery. Once I managed to say I'd like to be working for my Uncle Joe. Now Uncle Joe was a prison warden at a penitentiary where prisoners wore the ball and chain out on duty. Home folks got the message.

Representatives from Geneva Conference came into our camp. Jap leadership had not registered us with them until recently. The Japs said for over two and a half years that we were under the status of captured men and did not deserve Prisoner of War Status. We had obstructed their war plans they said.

When American forces began tearing the Japs up, they evidently saw the handwriting on the wall and became somewhat more considerate. As a result, the men from Geneva Conference were there. Of course the Japs put on a show for them.

A pig and other desirable fare was being prepared in our kitchen. When those visitors left, the Japs feasted but the inspectors got the message in other ways. Prisoners who were literally skin and bones walking around didn't have to say anything. Some of us made it a point to shake hands with them as they passed and leave written notes. Factory life didn't change much either.

A stash of pure grain alcohol was discovered by some prisoner out at one of the factory warehouses. If that Jap money had had any value at all the prisoners could have made a mint. Needless to say, every man working at MKK immediately began wearing a canteen on his belt. Evenings and nights got louder and louder until the Japs sent in a search group and broke up the party. A few fellows, one or two that I knew, had their canteens over at Jimmy the Wops' shop where no one ever found out. We managed to pick up two or three more at places where someone threw them out of windows.

Another menace turned up that the Japs couldn't figure out. Some prisoner recognized a plant growing along the road to and from work. He brought some into camp and the outlaw element in our barrack experimented some. Yes, it was marijuana and soon our barracks was reeking like a hippie haven. At one time or another most of us were puffing on those stalks. But I didn't inhale.

As a result of this nuisance someone broke out an old American flag that had been carried from Bataan around his body. It had only thirteen stars but that made no difference whatever. Men were marching around it, pledging allegiance, saluting, crying and celebrating. Right then prisoners couldn't have cared less that we were about to be charged with treason and several other worse crimes, because a guard was forced to present arms and got his ass kicked out. Some of those dumb guards didn't have ammunition and were short of marbles. We could easily dominate them on these rare occasions. What a weekend!

In less than ten minutes the Jap camp commander had called out the militia. By that time all prisoners were at their appointed places pretending to be sober. One or two privates sneaked out back and took refuge in Jimmy's shop. Those two people made sure they were seen repairing a hand railing on a building near Jap headquarters. Not many would believe the severe punishment that those in that barrack suffered. They were fortunate to have been only clubbed, beaten, stood attention all night and fasted on bread (small pieces) and water three days. Two workers seen repairing the railing were excused but ostracized by the rest of them.

That was the nearest thing to Old Glory we'd seen in a while and having it strung up there in that stairwell made America bloom in the midst of a desert. Enemies can kill Americans but they can't take America out of them. Looking back, it was well worth what it cost. After a few joints of that strange herb, who cared what happened? Being manhandled and insulted with gun butts and prodded with bayonets from time to time left scars those of us who survived are somewhat proud of when the doctors examine us. Sometimes we even remember what caused the small scars. Always we remember the reruns of our flashbacks when we relive yesterday. That day was one never to be forgotten. The Japs helped to impress the magnificence of such a moment into American hungry hearts. We had our day and the honor and grandeur of it will remain in our hearts till death. We thought they'd kill us all but there comes a time when dedication is more imperative than submissiveness, even unto death.

37

Factory Things

Spring of 1944 had just begun to warm sheltered corners guarded from brisk chilly winds. Sunshine began sneaking in about ten or eleven o'clock and Jap guards stole a few minutes of warmth behind piles of steel in back of the huge machine shop where many of us prisoners worked. By noon, most of the frigid shadows had thawed out.

Inside the shop we needed a little gasoline to start a diesel motor. I went outside to begin testing some of the barrels that sat around, hoping to find a quart or two. I would shake a barrel and listen, move to another and check. Jap guards were watching. I found a prospective one and removed the plug. Fumes came out. I patted my shirt pocket then my jeans as I peered into the barrel. One Jap guard volunteered his matches. I nodded and walked back into the shop. I was gone when he struck his match and peered into the small opening. It exploded but I was out of sight. I couldn't help it if a Jap did something silly and got blown to kingdom come.

Prisoners were always alert for opportunities to continue fighting the war. It wouldn't win the war but it reminded us which side we were on. When an overhead crane went out of control and smashed machinery you could bet it happened right after twelve thirty. Japs had just returned from lunch and prisoners had had access to controls, which might have been rigged.

If a factory burned, it would be at night when prisoners were in bed or possibly peeping out a window expecting to see fire.

According to the Japs there was some sabotage activity being carried out by the Chinese underground. Sorry China.

Larry, a friend who worked at another place, told me about one incident that happened at an overhead crane factory where he worked. Itchi Bon was owner-operator of the business. In Japanese "Itchi" means "one" and "bon" means, "number". So, Itchi Bon was "number one" in that establishment. They called him that. He promised the prisoners a good midday meal if they would come and put his plant back into production. The Chinese who once ran it starved and died out.

Americans can solve problems if they're given a chance. The prisoners came up with some productive ideas for Itchi Bon but Itchi Bon didn't follow through on his part of the bargain. The prisoners were turning out a large, overhead crane system on an average of once a week. Itchi Bon had a lot of advance orders for his cranes. Prisoners knew they would hold together until they were installed and the first load lifted. A professional welder made sure the welding looked perfect, but was not deep enough to endure. Others covered it with a perfect paint job. Itchi Bon sold them but he didn't feed the prisoners their promised lunch.

Outside the factory was an electric high voltage station. On the wall inside was an old fashioned electric switch that brought in enough current to operate welders and other machinery that were all voltage hogs.

At one time a safe switch handle had been on the switch but had long since worn away. Itchi Bon regularly picked up a wooden handle with a metal crook on its end and threw the switch off at twelve o'clock then back on at twelve thirty. In between, he went and had his lunch, came back belching and picking his teeth. Prisoners sat around the wall during that intermission, hungry and hating Itchi Bon for his lies.

A prisoner they called Blackie had been an electrical worker before the war. It was highly unusual to see that young man do anything constructive during rest period. That one day, Blackie was busy hosing down the floor. He examined Itchi Bon's handle at length and then replaced it where it had been. No one asked him any questions as he sat down.

When Itchi Bon threw the high voltage switch that day at twelve thirty o'clock he wrote his own obituary. He stood for a moment rigid as steel. Some smoke curled up around his hands. Then he fell into a liar's reward.

Japanese investigators came in and looked the scene over. They seemed to think Itchi Bon's ignorant practices had been his downfall. Even as they handled his stick, which was charred badly, they only shook their puzzled heads and walked away. They had no clue that Blackie had made a deep pencil mark all the way down the handle that Itchi Bon used. Pencil lead is graphite and graphite is an excellent conductor of electricity. The pencil mark triggered a high voltage surge. No one drew any out of work compensation when the factory went out of business, but America had won a small portion of the war and some prisoners had taken another punch at the enemy. We had to do it that way every chance we got.

Most of the fellows found some way to do their thing. Usually they were not as dramatic as Blackie's experience but managed to do some little something for America.

I knew two fellows who worked at the big MK factory that managed to somehow get a Jap guard across a barrel and they blackmailed him into bringing food in to them. They were careful not to overdo it and kill the goose that laid the golden egg. Just one nice bribe could mean continual blackmail.

There was quite a bit of whisper about how one man pulled a big operation off in the bearing department. He was an alloy specialist working at Timken Bearing Co. before the war. This bearing man used some method to make Jap plane bearings worthless after only a few hours of use. Jap pilots were bailing out of their dead planes far away from their bases. He knew.

American workers were capable of thinking and reasoning for themselves. They found courage to take necessary chances when need arose. Japs were good at doing what they were told if they had been told how, however they dared not do something unless they had orders. Americans took the initiative and were quick to seize the slightest opportunities to inconvenience or sabotage, even destroy Jap property or interests. As I look back on it, to protect themselves, the Japs should have at least kept us under fence until we died because we kept fighting our part of the war to the very end the best we could.

I wish I could share more of the tasks we undertook but seldom did one prisoner tell or brag of chances he had taken or missions accomplished. When I try, words just refuse to be said. You've heard that veterans don't talk about war unless they get drunk. It is one of the saddest things one can try. How do you think I'm writing this? I'm trying because I'm convinced that Americans ought to know history that has been locked up in hearts for the past half century. I want my own children, grandchildren and young ones of coming generations to know and accept Bataan History from the eyes that beheld it.

38

When the Tide Turned

One wonderful day several months before the war ended, two large bombers looking like American power, cruised across Manchuria. That was in North China, on the outskirts of Jap territory, not too far from Japan itself. Those bombers acted like they owned that air up there. Just think what that did to a thousand American prisoners down below who had been waiting to see America return for three and a half years! Just any good news would have about blown a fuse but this was jumping up and down hollering happiness. We'd kept the faith, knew it would happen sometime whether we were alive to see it or not. There it was!!!

At the factories next day the Japs were jabbering to each other about that experience. We listened. They said Zero fighters went up after them. One Jap was excited and said, "Those B-nee-ku-q's (B29's) just turned on another engine and went right straight up." At least one other Jap voiced his fears because their Zero fighters, that were supposed to be much better than anything America had, couldn't reach them.

That American scouting trip dotted all i's and crossed all t's in the last chapter of our prison story. We knew this was the beginning of the end for Imperial Japan. Time went by. I guess it was March or April of 1945 but still very cold in North China when the town of Mukden got bombed. One Sunday afternoon sirens started screaming in our camp. As we prisoners cleared the barracks the same orchestra was playing as far as we could hear. We spread out all over the parade field, which was frozen hard as concrete and cold as ice. I have no idea where the Japs were but I'd bet a bunch they were piled up underground somewhere back there.

Then we saw them coming. Can a person imagine the greatest thrill of a prisoner's life, not having been there? A hundred or more B29's in close formation were coming up toward us with vapor trails flowing out behind them. Just the sound reminded us they meant business, dangerous business. I can still almost hear that heavy drone, a hundred bombers making one sound.

I recall how a subtle fear gripped me, yet I was perfectly willing to take my chance with those Americans looking down through bomb sights toward us on the parade field that wonderful, terrible day.

I was lying on my back looking up at that crucial procedure. A more glorious sight I would never hope to see unless it would be the Second Coming of Jesus Christ. A more dangerous spot to be in one could never imagine.

As I watched I suddenly saw small shining objects being loosed from them. I can't explain how I felt when I knew in a few moments those bombs would do their job, whatever that was. Shortly they were swishing down and every moment seemed like an eternity. No, my whole life didn't flash before me. It was enough just trying to deal with the present when Mukden started exploding.

Factories half-vanished. Across the wall from us an ammunition plant that had anti-aircraft guns on its top had one-and-a-half walls left standing. Targets on past the airport were polished off and it wasn't half over yet.

Right when we thought they were going home they circled and came back that same run they had made initially. I was still watching those babies and wondering what they could possibly do this time that they hadn't the first time. Just as they approached, one pulled out of formation a little and I saw those small bright objects trickle out. I knew those were ours. I turned over on my stomach. Death was just a few breaths away from someone. Then I heard them swishing and the earth seemed to explode.

A B29 bomber, the Japanese Zeros could not touch them.

Three bombs landed in our camp. One hit the tall brick wall and threw shrapnel all over the field where we lay. Another blew the latrine end off barrack #3. An area on the low end of our field where garbage was burned was blasted by the third bomb. Twenty men were killed instantly and approximately a hundred were wounded badly. I was bleeding at only two small places. Afterward we were told they had our camp on their map as a plane assembly plant.

For several critical hours every able-bodied man in camp was involved in caring for the wounded. We carried them to the hospital, six men to a blanket. Two doctors, an American and a Jap, were doing their best professionally on that shrapnel riddled group of men who were screaming, praying and begging for help. Lack of bandages, medicine and other supplies hindered progress but they got by somehow. They worked throughout the night.

Three or four weeks after the bombing, I met an old friend walking across the yard. He was just out of the hospital. His right sleeve was tucked into his belt. I commented my sincere regrets.

"Oh, I've got another one here, besides, I was left-handed anyway," he calmly stated as he walked away. What an American!

The Japs were severely injured also. Their pride and dignity had bottomed out like an elevator. El Toro "The Bull" took his whipping out on us that night. He made it plain that he was in charge of us to the bitter end. Three hours of agony was exacted of us prisoners standing at attention in 0° Fahrenheit which left us with frostbitten feet and noses but we still glowed inside with the glory of that day's victory.

I heard comments: "I'll see you dead and in hell before I bow to you again." Similar declarations were made, demonstrating that America had been down inside all of the grief and suffering and like dynamite would explode one day when the fuse was lit. Those bombs had lit the fuse. America was back.

No matter what death an American dies, he still dies an American.

The Great Wall of China, a highlight on the truck ride to work.

39

Across Town

A little more than a month after we were bombed, a hundred and ten of us prisoners were transferred to a small camp across town. Those already there were mostly workers from another factory that had gone out of business. The facility we were to live in was fairly decent compared to some places we had been.

I rather enjoyed the truck trip. Just seeing the old China Wall amazed me. I had read about it but to look with awe upon it, one begins to feel an unexplainable mood of antiquity and mystique. An aura of its prehistoric glory brought thoughts of a China that had been robbed of itself by Japanese enslavement. The great wall had lost its first purpose, protection. As we traveled through its portal into Old Wall City, some of China was there still for the seeing but not very functional.

Jap factories had drifted into hard times. Their best Chinese workers and job leaders became incapacitated. The next generations were uneducated as well as being untrustworthy. Chinese would not talk about their circumstances.

Prisoners were divided into three work crews for three different factories. Two of us who had worked for "Jimmy the Wop" were now off-bearers in a large lumber mill. There was a carriage that carried the log controlled by the Sawyer. A huge band saw would cut a plank off the log each time the carriage came back and forth. We used picks to pull the plank of lumber onto rollers and shove it on to the next station in the process.

A pro-Jap Chinaman was the sawyer at the controls. The faster he caused the carriage to roll the more production he gave the Japs. He could work us prisoners to death and was probably expected to. A few days like that and I figured it was time to do something. When the carriage started back toward him on a speed run I kicked a large splinter, six or eight feet long under the carriage. It went like an arrow and missed the man by only a few inches. I didn't know how badly it scared the sawyer but he got the word. It made a kinder, more gentle workman of him.

A majority of the Chinese people did only what was necessary to survive. In a very real sense they were Japanese slaves and received barely enough wages to live on, no matter how hard they worked. The Japs controlled China in that if one didn't work or got disabled he died a beggar's death. Along the roads and streets men sat and slowly died without food, striving to keep flies out of their mouth and eyes. The harder Japs pressed for production the more Chinese dropped out of the work force. That was the reason factories needed workers.

One of the saddest sights we saw was ten-year-old children marching six abreast in a long line toward some factory early each morning. Both boys and girls met the same fate.

"Comfort women," Chinese women used for sex, started in their teenage years. When these women bore children it was usually in a cold dark alley, alone. If she had paper she rolled the child up and cast it into a garbage pit. We never saw half-Jap, half-Chinese children. It was a painful subject but one Chinese old man told us, "After the Japs are gone, we will still be Chinese people."

Since the Chinese labor market had suffered such abuse and good workers were in demand, we prisoners were drafted to elevate production. A sawmill, a steel mill and a textile plant were our reasons for being across town. Some of us were recovered from Dr. Ishii's program.

We had reasons to defy the Imperial Japanese and we were mean enough to try it. Soon after we were settled at our new jobs, three of us, one at each plant, began plotting together on a wild scheme to escape. We each chose an elderly Chinese man that seemed to be trustworthy. Both Chinese and Americans spoke enough Nipponese language to communicate.

Our Chinese friends didn't ask questions. They simply brought back answers. None of them knew the other was a secret agent.

Reports were basically the same each day when we compared notes. No one else in camp knew of our plans.

We were three men who were willing to accept challenges with small percentage outcomes in sight. None of us would hesitate to do what was necessary in order to succeed in our plans, even at the cost of our lives. We shook hands on that.

One of our trio was a master sergeant who had once been a pilot in the US Air Force. Taking unnecessary chances had been his undoing. The other two of us had reputations that would make us candidates for a dare-devil mission.

According to our notes, three planes warmed up each morning at the airport, a mile away. Two of the planes were copies of American planes, which our pilot had flown. We knew where they were and the numbers on each, and we knew the time they pulled out of the hanger. It was our business to be certain of how long those planes sat and warmed up before they took off on morning patrol. From our notes we had memorized the safest route between our barrack and the airport.

Plans were made and rehashed until we were sure they were as error free as we could make them. We would not change unless something went haywire, at which time we would stick close together and communicate.

First, when the four o'clock Jap guard came in for bed check we intended to take him and use his rifle to seize the guardhouse by the gate. Two more sleepy guards would be there where automatic weapons were kept. Telephone lines were to be cut and power switched off, the gate locked and the keys destroyed. That should put us outside on the street with no imminent threat.

Next, on our twenty-minute trip to the airport we were to keep to the shadowy side of the street and use our weapons when necessary, letting nothing, nothing stop us. We expected very few people on the street at that time of morning.

On arriving at the airport we expected opposition but the element of surprise was a big factor in our favor. We meant to destroy two planes and any Japanese action we saw around the hangers.

Chinese had informed us that Peking now might be in the hands of Chiang Kai-shek and would be a friendly place. Our pilot figured we could hedge hop as far as our gasoline lasted in that direction and evade ground fire and search planes. If we ran out of fuel before we reached there we would belly in and pray, pray, pray.

I still believe our plans would have succeeded barring accident or unforeseen difficulties.

An official portrait of the Japanese Emperor Hirohito.
His radio speech marked the end of the war.

40

The Emperor's Speech

Logs weren't coming in by train the way they once had. Neither was much-needed war lumber going out from a mill that had three or more times the capability of its present production. Beneath the floor a complex of belts and wheels working off of a great electric motor automated the machinery upstairs. A saw-dust pit was also in the basement. Chinese peasants worked in and out of there. That was where we traded with the Chinese. They brought us small amounts of food which they hid in the sawdust at a designated spot.

Rumor grapevines began buzzing that Russia was coming down through Manchuria. They had an old score to settle with Japan. Jap guards started coming through our work area much more often. A strange tenseness was growing. Our escape plan went on hold. Tank traps were being dug in the streets. Unmistakable signs of impending battle appeared almost everywhere. We were both excited and somewhat afraid.

One noon it was my turn to go for a pail of drinking water which took me past the Jap guard shack. Obviously something crucial was in progress. Guards had their hats off and were partially bowed as if in prayer. Their Emperor was speaking on the radio. I eavesdropped. I could understand about half what he was saying. He definitely said the war was over. Japan had lost. He expected an orderly surrender to the first allies they encountered. Such manner of action would save hundreds of Japanese lives and would be the most honorable thing to do.

My bucket went one way. I went another till I got back to the prisoners with the message. They mocked me, called me a lying Rebel. There was more fear than rejoicing. Anything could happen in a crisis where a war had gone wrong and there was so much savage disappointment. We only hoped fear would overcome their hurt and anger.

Within the hour trucks loaded us up and transported us back to our base camp across town. When we arrived there, all factory workers were there. No one was talking much. Anxiety had set in. Japs still had guns and had set up machine guns in the four guard towers around our prison. Rumors had spread fast about prisoners being massacred somewhere. We stayed mostly inside.

Five men who had parachuted out of an American plane that day brought tidings to the prison authorities that Japan had surrendered and they had come to take over the American prisoners. That was several hours before the Emperor's speech and the Japs were angered. They threw them in jail after severely beating them. That afternoon all prisoners were assembled back in camp and the five American officers released from jail. They mingled amongst us and tried to answer our many questions. We were so eager to hear. One of the biggest news items was the Atomic Bombs used on Japan. It amazed us. Freedom was making progress. Some of us just might break the bonds that night and look around town a little. This was a point where anything could happen.

Word got around reminding us that we were Americans and we were not to stoop as low as the Japs had and take our revenge out on them. Most of them had disappeared anyway.

We had already established the fact that we were in charge now. Rifles and sabers as well as other momentoes had been hastily accumulated. These items would be collected each day everywhere Japanese were surrendering. Our fellows wouldn't stand short.

41

Sowing Wild Oats

We Ex-POW's were still cooped up in prison when officially the war was over, and had been for two days. The way some of us figured it, if one is free, he ought to be free and we made plans to sneak out of camp shortly after dark. Camp was still officially closed and the town of Mukden was off limits. But there was no one to keep us from it. Jap authority was over and gone. There was no American commandant.

It wasn't hard to dig under the wire fence, then the water tile under the large brick wall was large enough to belly through. That put four of us on the prowl into Old Wall City. We had nothing specific planned, just sashaying around declaring ourselves.

Danger never caused us a thought, although at times there would be a burst of machine gun fire somewhere in the area. A few rounds of rifle fire intermittently broke the silence. Walking along the street we stepped across a dead Jap's body now and then, and ducked when a rifle bullet whined off a nearby post or wall.

Four men felt perfectly at ease in a strange, dark neighborhood where Russian troops were mopping up a Japanese section of town. It wasn't bravery that made us oblivious to the danger about us. It was just a hunger for excitement, a response to challenge, and I suspect, a prolonged war apathy. As a matter of fact, irresponsibility makes a dangerous adversary more dangerous.

A poster from the United States War Information Office informing Americans that the Chinese people were also fighting for freedom.

Illustration from the Northwestern University Library's World War II Poster Collection

Chinese people were poor but had done what little they could for us prisoners, like a few bits to eat now and then. This night on the town saw them sneaking into abandoned Jap houses and obtaining articles they wanted or needed. Jap overlords had kept the Chinese dry-cleaned and poor for years and we were sympathetic. No one asked us, didn't even suggest it, but we helped some Chinese loot abandoned Jap houses. After all, the Japs wouldn't be back. Jap sake wasn't much of a drink but we had all we would, drank to twenty or thirty celebrating Asians, both male and female. We were happy together for a few hours.

I don't remember where we got the rickshaws that brought us back to camp but we made it back and used our escape route getting in. Never again in a lifetime would all the thrills and possibilities present themselves just for the taking without any restraints.

After the Russians came in the following day, they opened the gate and the town to us, told us to take some and leave some. Four of us prisoners rested and knew we already had done that We might even try it again tomorrow, or the next day, or both. The fighting on the other side of the great wall was over now and at least some of the challenge was gone. By noon next day business ladies would have signs all over the city pointing to "cat" houses newly opened. Jap articles, curios, and mementos would be displayed by enterprising Chinese. Things would be different now until the Russian Communists established their regime. Chinese soldiers were already exchanging uniforms for Communist uniforms. It would take China fifty years or longer to become a great power, in spite of Russia. But China was ready to start.

I had no idea what it meant but I spent about an hour in a small hidden room with nine Chinese young men. Part of them were wearing the Chinese uniform and the others Communist uniforms. These soldiers were friends and accepted me as a friend after I was introduced to them by the lady of the house, as a former Prisoner of War, an American who was "ding-howa" (Very good – acceptable – safe). We shook hands heartily as I left them and called each other friends. That was three nights after the Russians secured the area. I hesitate to admit that this experience happened in a red light district and three other guys and I were there browsing around seeing what they were trading on.

I have often wondered what happened to those fine young soldiers? I also wondered how many of them had been hidden in Old Wall City and Japan had no clue at all?

The husband and owner of the house and I had worked together at the sawmill and he was my secret agent who gathered information for me. I found out that this Chinese friend knew what was about to happen much better than I thought. It was a friendly place, very congenial people.

Franklin D. Roosevelt, General MacArthur, Admiral Nimitz,
and Laehy in Waikiki, Hawaii —tying up loose ends.

42

Our Last Month in Mukden

Most of us were hanging around camp just waiting for something to happen, anything. We anxiously wished America would show somehow. There wasn't anybody holding their breath but our country was way over due to say, "Hello, boys."

A large plane circled our camp twice and it didn't have a Jap flaming sun on its side. Then it came in low, low like it would knock every smokestack in Manchuria down. When it got over us it gave us a salute with wing tips almost touching earth. He was speaking our language. I still choke up when I remember. It had been such a long, long time. But when America does something she does it big.

Some men were jumping up and down shouting what they felt inside. Some wished they could. Half-alive, half-dead human beings stood and knelt and celebrated every way they could, letting almost four years of hell on earth pour itself out in emotions that no man could fathom unless he had walked every step, felt every pain or experienced each emotion just the minute they exploded.

The whole weary accumulation of inhuman experiences culminated in this brief time. A frail prisoner sat over against a building with a blanket draped around his body. Color had faded from his face and wrinkles made it look like parchment. He was what one might call skin and bones. Someone shouted to him, "They have come! They have come! Aren't you glad?" Hoping to share the moment with him.

"Yes, I'm glad, but for so many of us, they've come too late," he halfway whispered and dropped his head.

It couldn't have been said better. That was the whole story. Too many thousands of our group lay in graves from the Philippines to North China and almost as many were suffering on the fence and could go either way, anytime. Sick men!

In a highly sentimental atmosphere things began happening American style in North China. Several acres of cleared land lay just across the wall of our prison and by radio, which the five men had brought in, some of our leaders were warned to keep that land clear. This initiated anxiety pains. Something was about to happen.

Large American bombers began bomb runs over that cleared land and Santa Claus took on a new meaning. Huge barn door like pallets were placed over bomb bay doors. Parachutes with loads of supplies were loaded on the pallets, all ready to be dumped for long neglected prisoners. One by one those bombers unloaded supplies that we so desperately needed but scared everyone within a half mile because of the swinging descent of the wooden frames or pallets coming down harum-scarum. No one knew where they would land. At this point in time no accidents could be tolerated.

Many of us hunted shelters where we felt secure and we stayed there until the last plane was unloaded and on its way back to Okinawa. Then it took hours to pick up the tons of goodies and move them inside the compound.

Anything that might in any-way interfere with my going home fever, I wanted to get far from. Those pallets and parachutes had no eyes or responsibility. I took a walk to distance myself from danger toward an old crane factory. I remembered a right pretty little Chinese young woman that lived over that way and we used to sneak a little wave to each other as we workers marched by her house going to work. I looked for her but didn't find her.

I was near the old factory wall when I heard a different sound coming toward me from over at the unloading zone.

Big planes dropping supplies.

The plane was hundreds of feet up when he unloaded and a parachute got tangled up and headed straight for me. I bellied down against the wall as a two-hundred pound missile hit directly over me. It sounded like a plane crash and scared the daylight out of me. Two containers burst asunder and covered my whole body. It was terrible. I began trying to work myself free from under that load. About two hundred pounds of shoes were a top me, along with the parachute and several buckets of tomato sauce splattered everywhere. I wasn't hurt badly but after I freed myself from under that load I was covered from head to toe with enough tomato sauce to do McDonald's for a week.

My new clothes were ruined. I got angry, awful angry. Then I sat down and laughed like a silly child. Wouldn't I look like I'd been through a paint factory when I came walking into camp? Actually they laughed for days about it. Those new clothes meant a lot to all of us. Brand new shoes we could keep spit shined and show off in. Creases in our new pants were sharp enough to cut a path to anywhere there was something happening. We were really dressed up for the first time in years. The supply room furnished a new suit and a shower prepared me to wear it. It was an oddball experience.

Russian contortionists entertained us one evening on a hurry up devised stage. I didn't know we were so hungry for belly laughs. I was sore for days.

Our own little string band gave us several hours of easy listening. Other ex-prisoners came up with talent, which hadn't surfaced in camp before. Skits were popular, funny speeches and other acts were put on the stage.

We found in one parachute load some contraptions that looked like they might be hooked together to make music. Some of the fellows who were good at that sort of things installed it in a building with a large speaker exploding recorded music all over the area. The most popular by far was a record, "Sentimental Journey." I believe it was the Andrews Sisters singing. That song did everything to a starved to death gang of prisoners that could have been done to get them ready for home. We couldn't weep even for joy. About all we could do at the time was tremble and crave, crave America that had been so-o-o-o long coming.

What a show they were putting on for us, the remnants of the "battling bastards of Bataan." Our cooks were working overtime preparing sumptuous banquets that we could only eat small portions of. Our appetites were much bigger than our stomachs, which had shrunk to a disgusting, inadequate organ that had been a long time disappointed. Our bodies, so bereft of America had become slaves to savage natures, educated by three-and-one-half years of serving savages' commands and being dominated by them. What could you expect us to be other than savages? Something to eat, something to drink and just a few other things was what concerned us most.

As I think back on the battles I have fought to climb toward an acceptable norm, I have struggled hardest, I guess, to find a level that would most honor my mother's prayers for me.

How the Chinese survived with any sense of identity, I don't know. Their humble hearts stir me deeply. It was hard to believe that one country could deliberately rape another as Japan did China. Japan robbed them of all their natural resources, closed their schools to keep them ignorant, took their businesses to keep them poor and their homes to make them slaves.

I remember child labor, disabled workers turned out to die alone, Chinese old women run down with Jap trucks as they attempted to cross the street.

I remember women standing on the street corners selling their small girls as slaves to anyone who had money. This was not out of cruelty but out of love. Any person who had money could give her girl child a better life than she could, a home, food.

Street people froze to death every night during cold winters and Jap trucks would haul them off to incinerators the next day. Families who owned a donkey were fortunate. They kept it in their shack at night and slept against it for warmth.

One could hear those single string, long necked violins screeching, almost every night somewhere out there in the communities saying we're mourning because one in our family has died.

Probably once in a year a marriage procession could be seen passing by. The only dress suit the groom would wear in his lifetime was a rental for that day only. His bride wore a plain white dress with small colored paper bows and flowers on it. They couldn't expect another celebration like this in their lifetime so they enjoyed a long column of neighbors and large paper dragons above them.

I've only touched the hem of poverty on the streets. If someone wants to see more they might try looking at the American prisoners, the latrines they died in, the mud holes where they were buried, the condition they came home in.

I've used some strong words describing the Japanese that I have known during WWII and my prison days. I have met several hundred over the world fifty or more years since that time.

My opinion has not changed in the least. The Japanese people have prospered as far as their industry and education

General MacArthur with the defeated Emperor Hirohito.
Rumor said that MacArthur had this picture taken and distributed
to show the Japanese people how small a man the Emperor really was.

can change their standard of living. But no matter how affluent people become, it doesn't necessarily change their nature.

I have talked to quite a few Ex-POW's and we all seem to be of the same mind. We have had more difficulty dealing with how General MacArthur abused us than with the Japanese. He displayed the most cruel, egotistical mind I have seen in any person in my life. I'm not alone in that assessment. Perhaps I can explain with one command MacArthur gave General Wainwright. "Fight till your last man is dead. Make as good a showing as possible." He never forgave General Wainwright for surrendering until well after the war was over.

43

No Guns Now

A s time went by, days into weeks, our moods changed from excitement into boredom. When an Ex-POW gets bored half way around the world from where he wants to be, the blues set in. Tempers were short fused. Patience nigh gone.

When you heard a few fellows saying, "I'll back you out," look for anything to happen. Little groups would unite and head out toward the big town expecting to drum up some sort of mischief. I just happened to remember there was a canteen of that grain alcohol hidden down at Jimmy the Wop's shop. Suddenly I had more friends than I'd ever had. We got some hours of forgetfulness without nightmares before the headaches started.

Mukden was about finished as far as entertainment was concerned. The ladies who ran the fun places already knew we Americans hadn't had a payday. So when the Russians came in and were not paying customers those madams just couldn't continue to do "gimmie" business so they went bankrupt. There ain't nothing more bankrupt than a cat house trying to run on fun.

Time just slow-poked by. During that month stay we did witness a number of men getting out of bed and into a uniform, not almost dead anymore. Oh, God what a miracle!

Some men who were well, started "feeling their oats" a little too much and wanted a fight with everybody. One or two took a good sound whipping home with them.

Then one day a barrel of Jap sake was brought out and someone used the butt of a Jap rifle to burst the top out of it. Fellows were using their canteen cups freely. About that time the loud speaker cut in with the message from one of our five new officers that our transportation was ready and waiting. There weren't many things we wanted to take with us. We'd been ready to go too long. Amidst considerable confusion we got under way. When the engineer started doing his professional thing with the big steam whistle, everybody's emotions overflowed. Those engineers, how do they do that?

Being under way going south was good enough. All other events on this trip would take second place to that. I simply just don't remember much that happened until we reached Port Arthur. Port Arthur was on the very southern portion of Manchuria. I think I must have completely relaxed for the first time since we became free.

When we saw that Red Cross ship sitting there, it cleared our minds of all doubt and we knew that finally, America had come for us. I couldn't help but remember what the poor fellow back in Mukden said, "But for so many of us they have come too late."

44

Typhoon

The USS *Hope* was an almost new and well-equipped ship for such a task. Some of the sailors told us they were just returning from Japan where they had taken a load of Jap prisoners home, then had orders to stop by south Manchuria and pick us up.

They were amazed at two things. One, they had never seen a group of men in such bad condition before. Two, so many of us had Japanese sabers belted around us. They coveted those souvenirs. They passed out tags for identification purposes and told us to pile our sabers in a certain area there. I didn't intend to do that. My saber was a memento that I no longer was subjected to that type of rule. I shed blood for the privilege to wear it. I risked my life to get it.

I balked and wouldn't give up my token of freedom. I wanted to see the Captain and was escorted by two capable looking chaps to his office. I saluted and explained that I wasn't meaning to be obnoxious or defying orders. I simply wanted his certification that I had left it with him to be picked up at the end of the voyage. He gave me a receipt and took my weapon.

My hunch proved out right. That pile of sabers got high graded—the best ones disappeared and their owners didn't know until they were ready to disembark. I collected mine from the Captain and it hangs today on my son's wall. No doubt one of my grandsons will own it some day.

USS Hope – *AH-7*
1944-1946

We hadn't reached Okinawa when a typhoon struck, one of the worst ones to ever hit that area. The USS *Hope* fought her greatest battle out there in the China Sea for over three days. Waves, we were told, broke eighty feet up, at times. A shipload of service men were in their greatest crisis. There's no way one could explain the anxiety we suffered, expecting any moment for that monster to take us down. No one aboard had seen as angry a sea, not even old sailors who were part of the crew. This was one of those times when each man had to take his life in his own hands every time he had to crawl to the latrine. Some of us took the ropes out of our barracks bag and leashed ourselves to our bunk. Many men were very sick. A few dry sandwiches made their way around twice or three times during those worst three days.

They told us afterward, we only lacked two or three degrees of sliding under. I figured we didn't lack much going airborne a few times as well. But as long as we could feel her tossing and bucking, hear her groaning and cracking we knew we were still riding. That little ship wallowed its way over an angry China Sea for three days. What a Captain!

What a Pilot! What a Ship! What a ride! What a frightful, helpless situation for a group of Ex-POW's to be caught in.

After the worst of the Devil Sea was spent and the storm began to subside some of us ventured on deck. Debris of every kind imaginable was riding those waves that still slapped over the deck occasionally. Parts of what must have been ships were afloat. The most amazing thing had to be those depth charges that had been anchored everywhere, floating by us. Two small armed vessels were shooting and exploding them.

A priest who was standing next to the rail was pointing to something with his left hand and crossing himself with his right. His features were aghast at some horrible thing. Then I saw it. One of those mines was on course right toward us. There wasn't any latrine nearby. I don't know how I acted. I almost passed out. I wasn't used to this kind of trouble and I don't know if a person can be or not. I had thought the danger was over. Then the USS *Hope* went into a spin at just the right moment to let that beast ride by. Shortly the tin cans exploded it. I'd have sworn at one time there it had our names on it.

One ship was towing another that had a hole in its side forty or fifty feet big. Then we saw one ship just floating along without anyone aboard. The side of something that had at one time been sunk I think, presented the "rising sun" in a very undignified fashion.

Yes, and some bodies, it looked like, at times showed for an instant and then gone. It's hard to deal with things that are so mind boggling, that have never happened before to you. Men that were in that typhoon still after fifty years recall it as their most memorable experience, their greatest moment of peril.

I took advantage of the situation for a fun ride I'll always remember. Seated on the deck with my legs locked around the pulpit at the bow and looking right down into the angry water which still tossed the ship about, I took a ride that would out-class a roller coaster. Down and down into the deep until waves seem to wrap around me, then power down there lifted us up and up a hundred feet in the air. It seemed like the ship was standing on her stern for a brief moment then the plunge again. From one side to the other she would shift as the bow sank again and again. What an experience! And no one told me how dangerous it was. At that time danger just didn't occur to me. I was free.

The island of Okinawa saw the last battle of the war. Japanese soldiers took cover in this church. What the fighting didn't damage, the typhoon did. Over 90% of all the standing structures on the island were destroyed.

45

Okinawa

We anchored and went ashore in Okinawa. There was where the last battle of the war was fought, and destruction left from that conflict was nothing as noticeable as what the typhoon had done. It had blown down everything that was up and soaked everything that was down. Men would cry if they had any tears left. Ships and boats bashed up on shore. Planes all broken loose from their anchors and rolled a hundred and more yards. Tent City (there were no permanent barracks) was flat and scattered far and wide from Main Street.

Some of the Air Force stationed there temporarily, were working hard to get up enough tents to accommodate themselves and us. Mess tents smelled like heaven. Amazing how they'd managed to come up with supplies and tools enough to do the job. We went directly to helping re-erect tents, giving a hand any place we could. Gasoline lanterns needed fuel and readied for night. A place to sit inside from the cool night air after we'd been fed well was all a person could ask for under the circumstances. Two days went by.

Only a few natives were beginning to come in out of the caves up in the hills. We all pitched in and cleaned debris from one runway. An old bomber came from somewhere and was made ready as a troop transport. Plank seats were added on both sides of bomb bay doors.

*In the aftermath of the fighting and storm, the Army made themselves comfortable
in a tent city complete with an outdoor barber shop.*

For once it was not name, rank and serial number. Those of
us who had been working hardest were loaded first. Takeoff
was breathtaking. Bomb bay doors were cracked open five or
six inches and we could look down. Acres of white crosses were
planted there below us in full sunshine. What a display of fallen
heroes. Thousands of tables were empty now all across America
because of the one battle. Sons, husbands and fathers were
down there.

More than one passenger wiped his sleeve across his face.
Ninety percent of us had our own battle scars, and I guess we
were all proud to have shed blood for America. But down there
lay the real heroes.

Just leave it to POW's to screw up. Three men had obtained
alcohol of some description and became obnoxious, pitching a
going home party. Two passed out and lay on the bomb bay
doors. One's curiosity caused him to find the bombadier's
compartment. Yes, he dumped his two buddies. They sobered
up fast. Their parachutes opened long before they traveled the

four miles down to sea. A small ship in that vicinity rescued two very sober Ex-POW's and a rather cowed, guilty-looking one up in the big plane got his butt kicked.

Crisis after crisis we POW's seemed to luck through. The pilot told us there was a storm in and around Manila and we'd have to land on the upper tip of Luzon. That was fine except that runway had never accommodated a bomber, wasn't built to. Was far too short. Nowhere else within range was there a possibility. The pilot gave us warning that those who were in the habit of praying, do the best job we'd ever done. Those who didn't, hold tight and at least try to think of something sacred because anything could happen. The pilot had all the stops down he had and his wheels were hitting seaweed long before he touched anything solid. Black marks stretched halfway down the runway. We got stopped right up against the hill in front of us, twenty yards past the runway end.

Imagine if you can what we were forced to endure before the days of nerve pills. Two nights were spent at the small Air Force Base there. Those people were so very congenial and shared

Acres of white crosses—the real heroes of the war in the Pacific.

the best they had with us but we had to move on. The pilot had that old bomber tied down backed up as close to the hill as possible and was revving it up until it was rattling and shaking to pieces it seemed. Then he turned her loose not sparing the fuel and as he came off the runway he lifted her just a mite. Seaweed hitting the wheels scared the devil out of us until we didn't hear it. Not until then were we sure we were airborne. I'll sail home next time.

This poor quality photograph captures the plight of Manila. It was one of the most fully destroyed city in the war. Much of the destruction was inflicted by the Japanese while celebrating the surrender of the American forces.

46

Back to Stateside

Manila looked much the same as we had seen her that day we sailed for Mukden, Manchuria three years ago. Buildings were full of shell holes, fifty caliber machine gun holes and the town was a shameful disaster. It looked the part of General Homma's first victory celebration just after Manila was declared an open city. War does ugly things to places and people. It leaves them that way.

Most of the vehicles on Manila streets were GI trucks and cars. Business places that used to flourish were either closed or the building used for something less valuable. There were no happy faces, no children playing as in olden times on the sidewalks. They were a people who had been caught in the middle between friend and foe and were left in distress.

Prisoners just arriving from Manchuria were trucked to an abandoned army base near Cavete, Santa Rosa. Nothing much was happening out there. All American vehicles though, had been alerted to stop for thumbers who had a long yellow string of POW markers on their sleeves. Big brass had said we could do just anything we were big enough to get by with, get it out of our system before we left for USA.

Red Cross ladies set up a small PX at our camp. We were issued coupons for cigarettes, beer and knick-knacks. When the coupons ran out we were sold things at a very reasonable price.

Santa Rosa was a small town but some people there knew that Americans were willing to buy what they wanted and arranged for that to be sold somewhere conveniently. There was a small theatre with Filipino pictures. A four-booth café sold short orders, very short. One twelve stool bar sold something they called beer. I seldom saw more than three or four customers except at evening happy hour. Two mediocre guitars and a darling singer were the entertainment. The singer was small in stature, wore a gardenia in her hair and a handkerchief in her crippled left hand. Graceful was definitely the way the girl moved about among the fellows. And sing, she was a natural with American songs that were somewhat outdated but they were the ones being sung when we left America. She brought the Ex-POW's in from 7:00 o'clock to 10:00 each night. They said she got prettier and prettier as the fellows drank that old McGill brew. She learned just how to play us guys too. I left some loneliness there and that was worth all it cost. I think that was why we returned each night.

During the month we lived there, we explored the whole Manila Bay area. Transportation was no problem and we knew how to hustle for ourselves. Accidentally dropping into forbidden places occasionally made prowling around exciting and worthwhile to a gang of men just out of prison.

Filipino people were very appreciative for the sacrifice we Americans had made, however, their economy had bottomed out and war had stripped them of their former ways of life and belongings. They knew we had some money in our pockets. Patriotism and greed was hard to distinguish between at times. Most Americans understood with some amount of pity because we had been with them through a crisis on the very bottom rung of life's ladder.

We would be departing for home, a land of plenty, and leaving these devastated and war ravaged people behind. Not in their lifetime would they ever know anything else.

Days sped by. Then one day it was time to go. I looked long and hard at their land and remembered the part I had played with our mutual foe. I was leaving them, taking with me only some scars and some memories that would always be a part of who I am.

A new, shiny ship on her maiden voyage waited at the dock. I don't know why I felt like crying as I walked aboard. I guess endings and beginnings both touch emotions. As we sailed out between Corregidor and Bataan, the feelings in my heart were bittersweet. Home was thousands of miles away but like a light at the end of a tunnel. It began to dominate my thinking altogether. America. Something like a wave swept over me. Pride because of the blood I had shed for her, pride because of my wonderful beginning years. That was the only home I had ever known.

Less than half way across the Pacific our new ship lost a motor and we limped on in. Patience is a luxury going half speed in the middle of the ocean when one has been away so-o-o long. In due time there it was, the big Bay Bridge up there over us. Going out under it was hell. Coming in set in motion feelings that had been suppressed and abused for four long years, a passion for home.

Docking in San Francisco didn't bring a passel of heartfelt memories. Like when we left we still didn't know what to expect. I reckon San Francisco is that sort of city. Uncle Sam had a variety of GI transportation that we loaded on to and were taken toward the big bridge to (I've forgotten) where we were lodged and fed.

Within the week, those who wished were taken over to Oakland to watch the Raiders whip Washington in a football game. It seemed rough enough but we didn't have to participate except yell if we felt like it.

Not many days passed until a group called the USO (I believe) invited us to a party. I don't know what they expected but it wasn't what they got. For a while some girls, pretty girls, brought us nonalcoholic punch and different kinds of doodads to eat. It was quite nice and was meant to be. Up to now we were enjoying it because it was the most lovely and delightful social function we could remember.

Some easy listening canned music opened up and girls began walking around where we were sitting. Some even asked us to dance. This was the first big disappointment, the worst embarrassment we had met coming home. Prison had robbed us of the coordination our feet needed for this endeavor. We didn't dare try.

At this point we weren't even good wallflowers and were thinking much worse of ourselves than we should have. One lady understood there was something wrong with communication there and in just a short conversation with us had everybody more at ease playing cards and other table games.

After we were back in our barrack my mind kept needling me about my chances of fitting in back home and how much adjustment I could make. I didn't want to disappoint my folks. Next morning I got drunk. A liquor store was a few blocks above us and I walked up there, got a fifth and started back. I guess it was a miracle I got back to the barrack because I drew a crowd.

I heard it was typical of San Francisco. A half dozen men were coming out of an alley and they just started walking up around me. Some wanted me to share my whiskey. Others were reaching to pocket areas trying to fleece me, begging and telling sad stories. One man was, I believe, taking up money for the widow of the Unknown Soldier. I'd never been propositioned in ways two of the group wanted me. A soldier driving an Army Command Car saw that I was in trouble and stopped. I'd never been so glad to get a ride, even for a few blocks. Being robbed was the least of my worries in that experience.

Worn and torn, a newspaper clipping showing T. Walter Middlton (far left) and other released Prisoners of War at the General Moore Army Hospital in North Carolina.

47

Homeward Bound

During our last week at San Francisco, all Ex-POWs went through a screening process of some kind that must have been regular routine. A dozen or more young doctors who spoke very little English made loud attempts at interviewing us. The more confused we got the more they yelled in some foreign language. We couldn't understand what they wanted. Their broken English was too broken. Confusion reigned on both sides of the desk. They had written on our records that we were uncooperative and paranoid. I don't know what else.

A question period with women behind a desk came next. One rather obese lady took the next three of us in line and attempted to gather information. We couldn't figure how the personal questions she asked could be of much medical or military advantage so we gave her a silent, stare treatment. She spoke in a coarse monotone, questioning our loyalty to America and our reputation as fighting men. One question was, "What would have happened to our country if all service men who got into a hard spot had thrown up their hands and surrendered?" At the point three men cursed her with vigor.

More inviting was the East Coast where my early memories were born. On the following day an army Sergeant came through bearing orders to fall out because our transportation was outside waiting.

Without hesitation everyone grabbed duffel bags, already packed, and began hurrying POW style toward Army trucks parked nearby. They got us to the train depot and didn't even wave goodbye. I can't think of any circumstances that would merit another trip back to Frisco.

In the dead of winter the train headed out the northern route across the US. Steam heat was a welcome commodity. One man asked a conductor how long that heat would last in case we got snow bound. Not many places along the way looked as if they had welcome mats out for a trainload of has-beens.

Tumbleweeds rolled and bounced across the prairie in front of a cold northern wind, stacking up in ditches and cuts where the train plowed through them. We saw no living creatures for what seemed like hundreds of miles. Things seemed so aimless out there. But I reckon the Creator had His own reason for its existence. I didn't hear anyone ask the price of land in that part of the country though. It was a tiresome trip. When we slept I dreamed about tumbling tumbleweeds.

We spent one night in that huge freight yard in Chicago. No one slept that night. The cars were bumping and jerking as they were switched up and down, back and forth. Some engineer had the crazies for tooting his horn constantly, all night long. About two or three cars would smash into each other and he'd give one big toot. A man couldn't lay still and there was no place to go. Dawn finally came. Soon they fetched breakfast. Yes, it was scrambled good.

The most important thing to me was two coaches of Ex-POWs heading south toward North Carolina and I was on one of them. That old going home feeling began to make music on my heartstrings that I didn't know were there. Once in a while though some small feelings of apprehension began hoboing into my happy memories, which made me wonder if home would ever be more than just a memory of what once was. I guess anxiety was beginning to do a job on me then.

Tired and troubled veterans were being more and more silent, too silent. That silence was saying that we all felt something none of us could say. Perhaps time would tell.

On November 4, 1945 our train just sort of sneaked in to a siding near Moore General Army Hospital, a few miles from Asheville, North Carolina. The train sat there popping off steam for at least an hour. It had brought one coach here with possibly forty patients. Arrangements had to be made at the hospital, they told us, for our admission.

It seemed like a mile that we had to walk before reaching the gate. Halls were long and steep at times, especially hard for us. There was no one to help us with our bags and many of the men were staggering, almost ready to fall.

Exhausted we trudged the last long hall to a large door where a man with a key said we were going. When the door opened and as we started in, we saw it. Mattresses lay on the floor. No cots. Walls were padded. Men began screaming, "Oh! My God, they've brought us home to put us in prison again." In just a few minutes we were incarcerated in the Psycho Ward of Moore General Army Hospital.

All hell broke loose but there was no one to hear us, no one on duty. Men were screaming and weeping. Some beat their heads on the floor. Others were maimed in various ways. The best I remember two men were dead. All night long it was a mad house with a few of us trying to quiet things down. I had experienced every horror trick the Japs had, but this was the most horrifying night of my life. So this was home!

It was one sad sight for the U.S. Army Officials to see the next day, what few that saw it. Men were crippled, bleeding, many out of their minds. If there was ever an angry mob of Ex-POWs ready to fight, kill or do anything to reverse this atrocity, it was us.

Large male nurses came in next morning in small groups patching up wounded men and doing everything possible to patch up relations. They were telling us they didn't mean for this to happen, that it was the only place they had to give a group this large with such short notice. One question we asked over and over, "Why did you lock the door? Why do you still keep it locked day and night you lying bastards?"

They began taking two or three men at a time before Army Officers for debriefing. On their return others went. Thirteen days passed and this process went on. No family. No phone. No

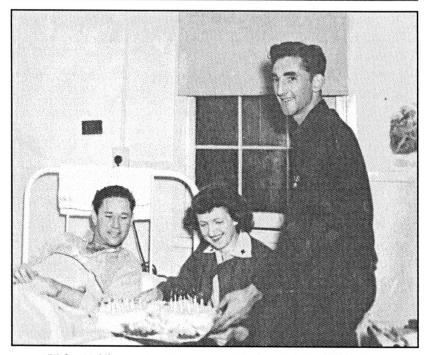

Walter Middleton and another ex-pow celebrating their birthday at Moore General Army Hospital during their first year back in the States.

radio. No paper. No contacts. No freedom. We thought our records from San Francisco had something to do with it. As I think back, this hostile treatment was due entirely to reports from San Francisco.

But word leaked out about our terrible treatment and it reached the right source or sources. Army bigwigs, inspectors, plain-clothed men that had authority written all over them were barking orders in every direction. A senator and other politicians came in asking serious questions about who was to blame for such a heinous crime.

On the thirteenth day we prisoners were released into barracks with other sick and injured soldiers. Relatives were notified. A solid hush-hush was clamped on the whole affair. Even the media was kept out. They didn't threaten us but they certainly made us know we'd better keep our mouths shut.

To show how eager the army was to get us off their hands, I'll tell my own experience. Others were the same as mine, just get them discharged and back to someone else's responsibility. I was on a doctor's ward whose passion it was to do just that. After I was his patient for approximately three weeks, he called me into his office and told me he was ordering me discharged. He explained what an honor it was to receive an honorable discharge and that I could walk out of that hospital a free man.

"But where can I go, Sir?" I asked.

"Anywhere you damned please," he said.

"What can I eat? Where can I sleep? I can't earn a penny. Who will take care of a person in my condition out there?"

"Oh, you're well. It will just take some time for you to get back to normal," he informed me.

"May I use your phone, Sir?"

"Why?" The doctor hastily asked.

"I need to call my Congressman."

"Look, I'll check your records and get back to you tomorrow. OK?" End of conversation. The following morning I was transferred to another ward and another doctor who was understanding in every way. I stayed a year on that ward, minus several two-week furloughs. People visited us there. All of our ills were doctored, our teeth repaired, the bullet taken out of my buttock. I was treated for amoebic dysentery and worms. X-rays of all kinds and other tests were taken. Medicine for stomach ulcers was prescribed.

During that time I was able to Americanize and emerge out of the savage existence I had been immersed in for almost four years. Little by little I began feeling like a human again. A better relationship grew with my family. Oh, how I tried to be acceptable and fit back into society. Through trials and failures I struggled. Growth was too gradual and my parents, I know now, were disappointed over and over.

Years of excessive anxiety, depression, and sickness of various kinds, kept me feeling insecure. Even the Veterans Administration kept giving me the lie, that they found nothing wrong with me. None of their doctors had ever heard of post-traumatic stress.

People, neighbors, were whispering, "Yes, he's in shell-shock. He's off a little. You can tell he's acting strange. He's wild as hell.

Moore General Army Hospital located outside of Asheville, N.C.

You know that ain't natural." I could hear it around and then I'd break my resolutions and get drunk again. With a double standback hangover I'd curse myself and make new resolutions.

Every month or so driving like a maniac I'd wreck my car again and come home all patched up. No one had an inkling the hell I was suffering at night. The Japs were still after me. I was seeing people die over and over. Flashbacks of those wartime atrocities plagued me until I wondered if I would ever whip these problems. No one knew how to help me. VA doctors did the best they could to address symptoms they hadn't studied in school. They just gave me pills and told me to go a-fishing.

One doctor told me, "Chief, you're going to have to do it the way you survived over there, alone and just a step at a time." I mulled that over in my mind and decided to take the first step.

After a few months had passed, those seven yellow POW hash-marks we wore on our left sleeve would open most any door for us at the hospital and in the closest town, Asheville, N.C. We were wild and post war America was liberal.

One thing we didn't like and we made it known was the German POWs who worked in the hospital. We looked to them for our evening passes and other important things. One ex-Jap prisoner beat one of them up, jumped all over him like a hen on a June-bug.

We outlasted the big push to discharge us and life became good at Moore General Hospital. I think just the slow leisurely system inclined us to heal. Our doctor on the ward where I was just about adopted us, treated us like we were his own boys, and there wasn't anything we wouldn't do for him. All of this was conducive to recovery. He said we were trying to find answers he didn't have, cures that weren't in the book. So, with a good doctor and fellows who were frank and open with him, we had the right kind of condition to recuperate, that made the trial and error years ahead somewhat easier, or more worth trying.

Most all of the fellows I knew were fighting different battles, had their own post-traumatic problems and were reacting to their own personal treatment over there. There was no buddy-buddy stuff amongst ex-prisoners. One thing for sure, we were all fighting to be free. Still fighting to be free!

I found a country girl, a virgin, and we fell in love. It was a new beginning and a far different challenge than I'd had before. She put it this way:

"Straighten up or we can't fit into a marriage relationship."

I straightened up and won her. I still had plenty of rough edges and bad habits to control but generally I was ready to take the next step. In the meantime, some good people got me in church and God did a miracle in me. I didn't feel pressure, just exhilaration. These new commitments made a measurable difference in my life.

A doctor at Moore General Hospital had told me back at one time there was a chance I could not have children but I got another surprise. We hadn't been married long when my wife became pregnant. Over a period of time, both a girl and a boy made us proud parents. I didn't know that life could be such a pleasure. It seemed that each day it took on new meaning.

Many notable things have evolved since those early post-war years. Making a comeback has been a delightful adventure. I'm being optimistic and trying to forget the painful memories, the wild midnight struggles and nightmares that invaded my peace and sleep.

It was a lengthy struggle through trial and error but I like to think I had Divine help to reach and maintain my reasonable potential. Many good people have made contributions, friends, family, acquaintances, even strangers have reached out a helping hand and given me acceptance and encouragement. I have found a wonderful support system among ordinary Americans who appreciate who I am and what I've done for the USA. I'd do it again for them!

Norman Rockwell's Four Freedom poster series produced by the Government Printing Office.

48

A Post War Revelation

I must clear up some misconceptions I ignorantly had during the depressing four months of war on Bataan.

Bataan was our little world, a strip of land fifteen or so miles long and we soldiers somehow got the mistaken idea that General Douglas MacArthur was running that war.

In the early chapters of this book I wrote my opinions, judgements and accusations concerning the general, as the evidence caused me to see and believe at that time. I had no understanding of what was going on outside our little area. That was history the way it appeared to the fighting men day after day in the heat of conflict.

A brief review of the Bataan predicament existing prior to our capture is in order.

We had not received more than a half ration of food since Japan started the Bataan Campaign. During the ensuing three months, our ration was twice more cut in half. MacArthur's soldiers were starving and fighting the best men that Japan could bring against us. We were fifteen to twenty pounds underweight with malnutrition and many diseases taking nearly half of the men off of the front. Not providing food and medicine for his men was, I believe, General MacArthur's first big mistake. I blamed him for that.

The General continually fed us hope that America was on the way with ships, planes and reinforcements and an abundance of provisions. We hung on every word of that until we saw that time was running out, that America had had sufficient time to at least attempt to get men and food to her besieged men if she intended to. I accused General MacArthur and I guess wrongfully so. I have cause to believe that at least one American High Official assured the General of this American pledge but not to our knowledge at that time.

General MacArthur evidently believed that and tried to do the best he could with what he had until help arrived. It didn't. We Engineers had built at least a half a dozen airfields that he had ordered built, hoping America would come through with planes. They didn't.

One habit the General had, was pumping up his own image on his daily radio broadcast to the American people. He took all of the honor and glory happening on Bataan and never mentioned his sick, hungry American troops who were fighting near the end of the battle for their lives or the sacrifice they were making.

Well over a half century latter some pertinent facts come out that show General MacArthur wasn't King of the Far East after all. But he did get some people clamoring for their hero over there to run for president against Roosevelt and Roosevelt was President of the US and commanding officer over General MacArthur. The Washington Bureaucracy went into the fast business session and changed some huge details like removing General MacArthur from his command of the Far East and putting him in exile in Australia until they might need him.

The Navy was officially given the New Offensive Leadership role in the Pacific and they bypassed the Phillipines erasing Bataan from their map and leaving America's honor in debt to those thousands who had fought to the bitter end trusting America's integrity. I don't blame anyone anymore.

Through the years I have decided that it is needless to try to understand America and the things she does. I am just one of the millions of people who are a part of her. If I didn't still love her and wasn't again willing to die for her, warts and all, I'd leave and go to some less worthy place. There is no place equal to her and I'm so proud I shed blood and bore lots of painful living for what she stands for in this world of ours.

My prayer is: "God bless America."

About the Author

T. Walter Middleton was born and raised in the Great Smoky Mountains near the Qualla Boundary (the Cherokee Indian Reservation). He is retired from the pastoral ministry, where he served churches in Jackson County, North Carolina, for almost half a century.

Mr. Middleton is a veteran of World War II, where he served in the Army. He was held as a Prisoner of War by the Japanese for three and a half years, first in the Philippines, and later in Mukden, Manchuria.

In the above photo, taken early in the year 2000, Walter Middleton shows off one of the few souvenirs he has from his war-years. A saber that belonged to the Camp Commander at Mukden.

T. Water Middleton lives with his wife, Sally, in Sylva, North Carolina. In 1998 he wrote the book *Qualla, Home of the Middle Cherokee Settlement*, which told the myths and stories passed down to him by his grandmother, Moriah, and other elders of the Cherokee people.

Also by
T. Walter Middleton

Qualla: Home of the Middle Cherokee Settlements

Tales of the Great Smoky Mountains' Native Americans

Until now, little has been written about the Middle Settlement Cherokees of the Qualla Boundary, the Cherokee Indians of the Great Smoky Mountains. Descendants of the "Principal People," these Native Americans come to life in stories and lore passed down through generations.

T. Walter Middleton gleaned many of these tales from his Cherokee grandmother and native elders who lived around his Smoky Mountain home. He traces the Cherokee race from their origins through the 20th century, touching on their religion, myths and legends.

6x9 Tradepaper, 288 pages, Full color cover with many interior photographs. ISBN 1-56664-136-5 **WorldComm**® $16.95 U.S. / $21.95 Canada

To order call: 800-472-0438. MasterCard & Visa accepted. Prices do not include shipping and handling. All prices subject to change without notice.

This and other titles are available from **Alexander Books**™ 65 Macedonia Road, Alexander, NC 28701. 828-255-8719 Order line: 800-472-0438. Visit us on the worldwide web at: **http://www.abooks.com** Safe, secure on-line shopping.

Printed in the United States
54168LVS00005B/307-324

9 781570 900976